Getting the most from your COMPUTER

a practical guide for
older home users

Jackie Sherman

BOOKS

© 2002 Jackie Sherman

Published by Age Concern England
1268 London Road
London SW16 4ER

First published 2002

Editor   Ro Lyon
Production   Vinnette Marshall
Design and typesetting   GreenGate Publishing Services
Printed in Great Britain by Bell & Bain Ltd, Glasgow

A catalogue record for this book is available from the British Library

ISBN 0–86242–346–5

Whilst the advice and information contained in this book is believed to be true and accurate at the time of going to press, neither Age Concern England nor the author can accept any legal responsibility or liability for any errors or omissions that may be made. Please note that while the agencies or products mentioned in this book are known to Age Concern, inclusion here does not constitute a recommendation by Age Concern for any particular product, agency or service.

Bulk orders
Age Concern England is pleased to offer customised editions of all its titles to UK companies, institutions or other organisations wishing to make a bulk purchase. For further information, please contact the Publishing Department at the address on this page. Tel: 020 8765 7200. Fax: 020 8765 7211. Email: books@ace.org.uk

Contents

About the author

Jackie is currently teaching IT to adults at Oxford College of Further Education and in a local community education centre. She also writes computer course materials for distance learning colleges and answers IT queries for various Web sites and magazines aimed at the over 50s.

Jackie graduated in Zoology from Oxford University and worked for the British Council in Ethiopia. She then joined the CBI to work in the education department, before spending 12 years as a university careers adviser. After training as a school teacher she became involved with several educational research projects before moving into adult basic skills and computers.

Her first book, *Basic Computer Skills Made Simple*, was published by Butterworth-Heinemann in February 2001.

Acknowledgements

To Graham, William, Toby and Beryl for all their support.

Using this book

This book aims to enable you to enjoy your computer more and to save time. Books can never take the place of a personal tutor, and so the ideal is to find a local IT class that you can attend to get you started. This book can then be used to support and extend your learning, and for reference if you get stuck trying to carry out an activity on your own at home.

It is likely that many of you reading this book will not be completely new to computers. Research shows that the assumption that most people who are over 50 and interested in learning about computers have never used a computer before is incorrect. You may well have used one at work, perhaps gaining some experience with one software package, or you may have observed grandchildren or other relatives using one at home, and may even have bought a computer but not yet learnt how to use it fully.

For those of you in this situation, it is hoped that this book will be especially valuable. Not only will it introduce you to the basic aspects of applications you may not have come across before, but it will also show you how to develop your skills and use the more advanced features of familiar software packages. You will also be shown how to make use of the integrated aspects of programs so that drawings or charts produced in one application can be attached to emails or copied across and added to separate documents to create even more sophisticated and attractive pieces of work.

Each chapter looks at one of the main uses for a computer and takes you through an introduction to the basic skills required before moving on to useful and enjoyable projects such as creating greetings cards, attaching files to emails, finding a tutorial on the Web or producing charts. In the chapters on word processing, spreadsheets and presentations you will also find summaries of operations in the form of checklists.

The detailed instructions are based on PCs running Windows 98 as the operating system and using the software suite Microsoft Office 2000 (which includes Word for word processing, Excel for spreadsheets and PowerPoint for presentations). There are so many similarities between these and slightly earlier or later versions that you should find it quite straightforward to apply the advice in this book even if you have Microsoft Office 97 or are running Windows 95, ME, or XP. Most of the menus and commands that are in these applications are very similar to those in Microsoft Office 2000. Occasionally we have included some screens from Office XP to indicate some of the differences.

A glossary is provided to explain technical terms and there is an index at the end to help you find your way around the book.

All menu options are shown in type like this.

Introduction – why bother with computers?

Computers are not only for the young, nor are they a luxury that older people can well do without. People over 50, whether they are retired or not, have a wide range of interests and 'Information Technology' can help in many ways, including:

- If you are involved with any local clubs or societies, or you give the occasional talk, you can use your computer. For example you can build up a database of members' names and addresses; produce attractive publicity material or a newsletter; and simplify sending letters out using the mail merge facilities. You can also create professional-looking documents, charts, slides or even computerised presentations.
- If you are housebound or find it hard to meet people, yet want to make contact with others having similar interests and hobbies – or if you simply want to keep in touch with friends and family – you can register for an email address to send your messages electronically, or you can use chat rooms and newsgroups to pick up useful hints or exchange ideas.
- Should you find shopping too tiring or want to check out the cheapest prices, you can browse the 'virtual' aisles of online supermarkets, select goods and organise home delivery via the Internet, and compare offers before buying almost anything online.
- If you want to save money and be creative at the same time, you can make your own greetings cards, notelets, business cards or headed paper for example.
- You can learn something new – take a course online, or buy a do-it-yourself CD-ROM, on a topic such as interior design or garden planning.

- If you want to sell things or advertise your services it is quite easy to set up a Web site to promote your business, or use desktop publishing facilities to produce advertisements, posters or flyers.
- For anyone who likes music, it is simple to 'download' sounds or sheet music from the Internet, listen to recordings before you buy or simply read reviews in online magazines and newspapers.
- Finding information on anything from train timetables to hotels, art exhibitions, local evening classes, the weather, recipes, knitting patterns, films or spare parts for your lawnmower is so easy with a computer – you just need to surf the World Wide Web.

Finally, if you don't want to feel left out or find you are unable to make use of new technology when so many organisations, including banks and government departments, are moving their operations to the Internet, then this is another good reason to learn how to use a computer.

Will it be difficult?

When you haven't learned anything new for a while, or don't feel you are particularly good with 'machines', you may worry that computers are going to be too difficult or technical to master. Yet adult education classes are full of mature students happily getting to grips with word processing or 'surfing' the Web and sending emails. It is clear from the numbers of older people attending computing classes that age is not a problem. Some of the fastest, most enthusiastic and successful learners are in their 50s and 60s or older. Good learners, however, do seem to have certain characteristics in common:

- they feel able to make mistakes and learn from them;
- they are willing to read and follow instructions;
- they are prepared to 'have a go'; and
- they are quite content to learn at their own pace and take things a step at a time.

Although it can slow you down if you forget what you did last week, you don't have to have a good memory to succeed with computers. Keeping your own notes, referring to books, and getting help from the computer itself via the help menus, all mean that you don't need to worry too much if you forget how to carry out a particular task. In most of the programs, you can even find out which button does what by resting the mouse pointer on the button and waiting for the description (known as a 'screen tip') to appear.

What you do need with any new skill is patience, and as older people often have this in abundance, there is no reason at all why anyone who wants to cannot learn to use a computer in a wide variety of ways.

What if you are disabled?

There are various pieces of equipment you can buy to overcome specific problems when working with your computer, including:

- foot and wrist rests;
- shaped keyboards;
- document holders;
- writing 'pens' or joystick controls;
- shaped seats;
- stands to alter the computer height;
- magnifiers to increase the size of everything viewed on the screen;
- voice recognition software that allows you to talk rather than type;
- speech synthesisers so that text can be 'read aloud' for people who have a visual impairment or it can be presented in Braille; and
- special keyboards or mice that can be operated with very limited hand or body movements or even replaced by a switch.

Within the various programs, you can increase the size of the text display or build up a range of words or phrases that can be inserted automatically, and you can even alter the speeds of mouse or keyboard strokes.

More information on adapting your computer in this way can be found on The Microsoft Accessibility and Disabilities Web site at http://microsoft.com/enable

For more serious disabilities, it is worth contacting organisations such as The Ability Net (PO Box 94, Warwick, Warwickshire, CV34 5WS. Tel: 0800 269545, www.abilitynet.co.uk). They can advise on the wealth of hardware and software solutions known as 'adaptive' and 'alternative' technologies now available to overcome any difficulties you may have.

How much will it cost?

If you haven't got your own computer and are thinking of buying one, a new computer for home use that can link to the Internet and run any of the applications you are likely to use will cost between £500 and £1,000 at the time of writing. For this you should get good sound and image quality, enough memory for running programs, a large capacity hard drive for storing programs and files, and a basic printer. Many retailers also include a modem and a 'bundle' of software programmes, although not necessarily Microsoft Office.

It starts to become more expensive if you want to use other hardware items such as:

■ a digital camera to convert your own photographs into computer files;
■ a scanner to copy book or magazine pages into the machine;
■ advanced colour or laser printers; or
■ a portable MP3 player (see page 141) to play music from the Internet.

To check out the best prices, you could consult the latest *Which* consumer guides in your local library, or buy one of the many PC magazines aimed at new computer users. A good one is *ComputerActive* as it comes out fortnightly and is written in 'plain English'.

Buying a computer

This is now something many people do via the Internet – you can use retailer sites to find out about deals but still use the telephone to place your order, or you can complete an order form and buy directly online. If you are not ready to do this, there are a number of high street stores that offer special deals, such as Argos, Dixons, Toys R Us, PC World and even on occasion supermarkets such as Tescos. You may prefer to buy a computer magazine in the newsagents and send for catalogues from computer manufacturers or specialist retailers, such as Dell or Evesham for example.

Although you can find second-hand computers advertised in local newspapers, they may not turn out to be economical in the longer term as their smaller memory and slower processing speed may prevent you making the most of today's software programs. Technology moves on so fast that you should also check that there is room to add further memory or extra hardware so that you can upgrade your machine when you need to.

Saving money

Once you start work, the main ongoing expenses you will incur are paper for your printouts, ink cartridges for your printer, and telephone charges when you connect to the Internet. In Chapter 7 you will find tips on keeping Internet phone charges low, and once you start creating your own headed paper, greetings cards or leaflets you can begin to see that computers could save you quite a bit of money. When you add to this a free 'yellow pages' service so that you can look up any business address or telephone number; no more stamps and envelopes when sending your mail electronically; newspapers and magazines online; being able to use the Web to compare prices and buy the cheapest holidays, theatre tickets or cars; and the availability of free tutorials on a range of subjects, you may wonder why you didn't start using a computer years ago.

Other options

If you aren't interested in owning a computer, there are places you can go to use equipment cheaply or for free. Check your local community groups, college, library or post office facilities, or call in to an Internet or cyber café where you can use a computer for a few pounds an hour and get a coffee at the same time.

Chapter 1

Working with a computer

There is a great deal of jargon surrounding Information Technology, and confusing things can happen when you are on your own using a machine. This chapter explains the basic facts about computers and introduces you to some of the technical terms you will meet later in the book. It covers:

- Hardware and software
- Parts of the computer
- Caring for your computer
- Your health and safety
- The Desktop (including using the mouse, the Start menu, turning the machine on and off and changing the settings)
- Working with windows

Hardware and software

At its simplest, 'hardware' refers to parts of the computer you can see and touch, such as the screen, cables, printer or mouse. 'Software' is the name given to any instructions, in the form of programs, that the computer needs to be able to work effectively.

Software can be stored in different places:

- inside your computer on the main disk (referred to as the hard disk or (C:) drive);
- on floppy disks that you buy in boxes of 10 or 20 that are inserted into the 3½" floppy (A:) drive; or
- on CD-ROMs that are placed on the slide-out tray in the (D:) drive (see Figure 1.1).

There are two main types of software:

1 'Systems' software – which includes the operating system (such as Windows) and programs controlling your hardware, for example the computer, mouse or printer. Most systems software is already present when you buy your computer, so that you can use your mouse or keyboard straightaway, but some may have to be installed, for example if you want to use a new digital camera.
2 'Applications' software – all the programs you use at your computer, such as word processing or drawing packages.

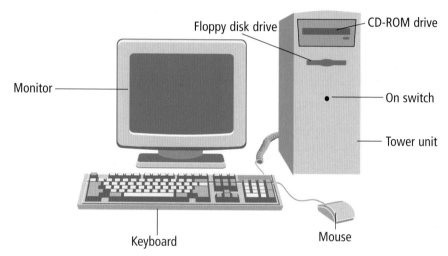

Figure 1.1

Parts of the computer

When you buy a computer, you will always need the basic hardware components: monitor (screen); mouse; desktop or tower unit housing the Central Processing Unit (CPU), memory (RAM) and hard disk; a keyboard; and a printer.

You may also want to include two other pieces of equipment:

- *Scanner*: these usually take the form of lidded boxes which house a moving light source under the glass. Place your text or picture face down on the glass, close the lid and use the program you have installed to scan the document. It will appear on your screen and you can edit it, select parts to copy into another document, save it onto your computer or print out a copy.

■ *Digital camera*: small and similar in appearance to normal cameras, these take pictures that are stored electronically. When plugged into your computer, you can view the pictures and select one or more to copy, save or print onto paper.

Computer 'space' is measured in bytes. If you are buying a computer, you should buy one with the biggest hard disk you can afford, so that there is enough room to store all your programs and files (files are the pieces of work, such as word-processed documents, that you create on your computer). Although the minimum requirement is 6–10 gigabytes (Gb), many systems are now supplied with around 40Gb.

For the most flexible way of working, you need at least 64–128 megabytes (Mb) of memory (RAM) as this allows you to work with sophisticated programs and carry out different tasks at the same time as well as speeding things up.

As with a TV, the size of the screen is down to personal choice but it is probably best to buy one that is at least 17 inches.

Caring for your computer

You don't need to worry too much about special precautions for looking after this expensive equipment, as normal housekeeping rules apply. In particular, it is sensible to keep food and liquids away from any electrical items, and floppy disks can be badly affected by dirt, heat or magnetism.

Unfortunately, when you use the Internet or borrow disks, you may introduce rogue programs known as 'viruses' that can badly affect your computer. To safeguard your machine, it is a good idea to ask the company that sells you a computer to include anti-virus software, or you can buy a program from a company such as Norton or McAfee, and you should follow any instructions to update this on a regular basis.

Your health and safety

One of the major problems with computers is that they are so addictive; you can spend hours on the machine without realising it. This can mean sitting in a cramped position straining your back, neck or wrists, or gripping the mouse too tightly for too long a period.

The answer is to set your computer workstation up properly and to do things in moderation. Don't sit for more than 30 minutes at a time before getting up and moving around. Try to hold the mouse lightly, and sit in a chair that supports your back and allows you to keep your eyes roughly level with the monitor and feet comfortably on the floor. Your arms should be level with the keyboard, and everything should be kept close to hand so that you aren't stretching awkwardly to reach the printer or documents you may be working from. If eyestrain or glare is a problem, you could draw the curtains or blinds or reposition the machine; stop working at any sign of a headache or distorted vision.

Most people can work happily with a computer if they take these sensible precautions, but you should always see a doctor or optician if you have persistent problems.

The Desktop

With Windows 98, after turning on the power and waiting for the computer to go through its setting up procedure, you will see an opening screen that has a coloured or patterned background. Various small pictures ('icons') will be visible, representing common objects in an office such as a waste paper basket (Recycle Bin), your machine (My Computer) and filing cabinet (My Documents) (see Figure 1.2).

Using the mouse

To send instructions to your computer, you can use either the keyboard or the mouse. Pressing keys is simple, but the mouse may take a while to master. If you roll the mouse gently around on its mat, you will see an arrow-shaped pointer move across the screen. With practice, you will be able to control this movement so that you can rest the pointer on any part of the screen. Press or 'click' the left mouse button to make your selection. Selected items usually change colour so that if you click the wrong item by mistake it will be quite clear and you can move the pointer and click again. Even if your clicking opens a window

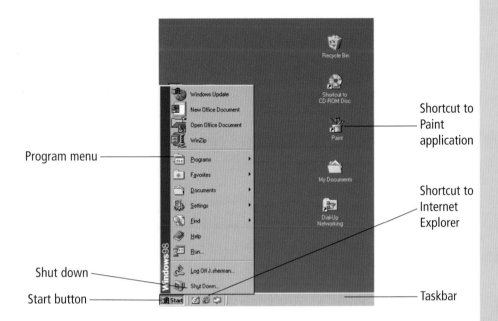

Program menu

Shortcut to Paint application

Shortcut to Internet Explorer

Shut down

Start button

Taskbar

Figure 1.2

you hadn't meant to, just close it (as explained in the section on working with windows on page 11) and try again.

Always click the *left* mouse button when opening or selecting items or carrying out the main computer activities. The *right* mouse button is used when you want to display a short menu of relevant options. Holding down the left button and then dragging the mouse across the mat will enable you to move objects on the screen or select text word by word.

Your mouse can be used for a number of activities, and the shape of the pointer when you use it determines the specific action. For example:

- Click an arrow and you can select a menu option or add a tick to a box.
- Click a vertical bar over text and you place an insertion point on the screen.
- Click a hand and you open a new page on the World Wide Web.

When the left mouse button is clicked twice very fast ('double-clicking'), it opens a program or file. (This action can be replaced by one click and then pressing Enter on the keyboard.) In a text document, double-clicking will select a word, and triple-clicking (ie three fast clicks) will select a paragraph.

The Start menu

The icons visible on the Desktop will vary depending on who first set up the computer. Each one represents a shortcut to a common program/application or file stored on your computer's hard disk, and in Chapter 2 (see page 22) you can find out how to create your own shortcuts to programs you use often. All your other programs are available via the **Start** button housed at the bottom of the screen on a grey taskbar.

To open any application, either 'double-click' the icon or click the **Start** button to open the **Start** menu. Roll your mouse up the menu to **Programs** and another menu will open. Slowly move the pointer across to this menu and click your chosen application.

Other useful features of the **Start** menu include:

- a list of recently opened files (click *Documents*);
- a *Run* option for starting up a CD-ROM or DVD; and
- a *Help* menu.

Turning the machine on and off

As you work, various temporary files will be created within the computer that will be sorted out automatically before your next session. To enable this process to take place, it is important to follow a systematic shut down procedure every time you finish work, rather than simply switch off.

To shut down properly, click the **Start** button at the bottom left of the screen to open the **Start** menu. Click **Shut down** and click the small round button next to the *Shut down* option and then click **OK** (see Figure 1.3). You may be reminded to save changes to any open files you have been working on. You will then be told that it is safe to turn off the power (or this will happen automatically).

Select appropriate option

Figure 1.3

If you do just switch off, next time you turn on the computer it will need to check the system thoroughly before you can see the Desktop, and this can take quite a few frustrating minutes.

Although not as drastic as turning the power off completely, you may need to restart the computer at some stage. This is because, on occasion, it seems to freeze up and either the mouse won't work or programs no longer open or close properly.

A quick way to bring it back to life is to hold down both the Ctrl and Alt keys (see page 27 for an introduction to the keyboard) with one hand and press the Delete key with the other. Doing this should open a window offering an **End Task** button that, if you click, will take you back to the Desktop where everything should work normally again.

If nothing happens, press the **Restart** button that should be close to the Power button on your machine, or – if the mouse is still working – select **Start** – **Shut down** – **Restart** and then wait for the machine to restart itself.

Changing the settings

There are various changes you can make to customise the features and settings on your computer. For example, if you position the pointer over an icon, click and hold down the *left* mouse button and roll your mouse around, you will be able to drag the icon to another position on the Desktop.

You can also change the background colour of the screen. To do this, you need to open the **Control Panel** or **Display Properties** box.

7

Open the **Start** menu and select **Settings – Control Panel** to see a list of items such as *Date/Time*, *Internet Options*, *Regional Settings* or *Sounds* (see Figure 1.4). Open any of these by double-clicking the icon and change the settings. For example, open *Mouse* and slow down the mouse double-click speed if you find it difficult to do this very quickly, or within *Keyboard* change the cursor flash speed if you want to see it more clearly (the cursor is the flashing black bar that marks the text insertion point).

There are many different ways to display window contents and you may see a list, or large icons, rather than the displays shown in this book. You can change window displays by selecting options from the View menu.

Change the window display

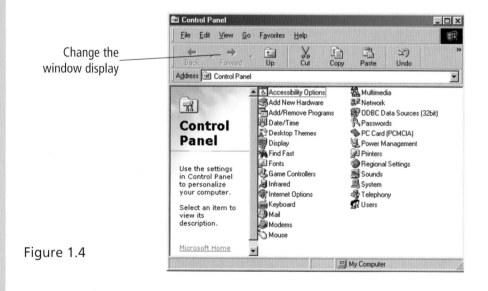

Figure 1.4

If you double-click *Display* , you will open a new window on the screen (see Figure 1.5). (Small windows – opened via a menu – that offer you various choices to click or type in are generally known as 'dialog boxes'.)

From the Display dialogue box you can click the tab at the top of the window that is labelled *Background* to preview and change the images (referred to as 'Wallpaper') or patterns on your Desktop. Select the tab labelled *Settings* to change the colour and resolution of your screen

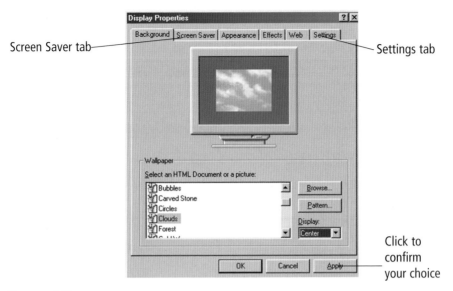

Screen Saver tab

Settings tab

Click to
confirm
your choice

Figure 1.5

(for example to make the screen area 640 × 480 so that images are at
their largest), or *Screen Saver* to run different moving images and set
the time delay before the computer goes into a power-saving mode
when you stop work for a while. Always click *Apply* to confirm your
choices before clicking the OK button.

From the Desktop, there is a shortcut to opening the Display properties box – *right*-click on an empty part of the Desktop and select
Properties from the menu that appears.

Working with windows

You will find that working with most of the programs available on a
computer means opening up a window on the screen. More than one
window can be open at a time and these can be resized or moved around.

Although each software application has its own particular menus and
shortcut toolbar buttons, there is a fundamental similarity between
them that helps when you move from one to another or learn to use
new programs. If you are new to Windows 98, try to familiarise yourself with the basic window design (see Figure 1.6) as the various
components will be mentioned many times throughout the book.

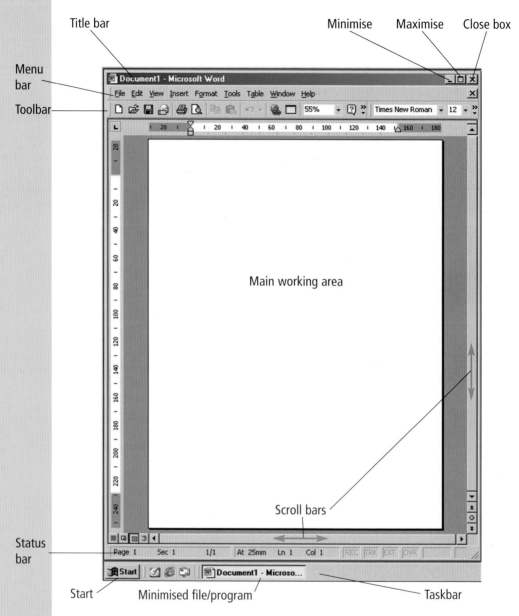

Title bar

Menu bar

Toolbar

Minimise   Maximise   Close box

Status bar

Start   Minimised file/program   Taskbar

Main working area

Scroll bars

Figure 1.6 (The parts of a window. The example here shows Microsoft Word, but the windows of other programs are similar)

The parts of the window are:

Title Bar:

This is blue when the window is 'active' (ie when it is the current one in which you are working). The name of the program and file shows at the top left and the resizing buttons show top right:

   🔲 Click this to minimise the window so that all you see is a labelled button on the taskbar. (You can reopen the file or program at any time, to become the active window, by clicking the labelled button once.)

   🔲 Restore (ie change) the window size so the Desktop can be seen behind it. In this mode, the window can be moved or resized.

Move a window: Click in the Title Bar, keep holding down the mouse button and then drag the window across the screen.

Resize a window: Click and drag a border in or out when the pointer moved over the border changes from a single white arrow to a black two-way arrow ⟷.

   🔲 Click to maximise the window to its largest size (this button alternates with the **Restore** button).

   ❎ Close the window – either a file or the program itself – by clicking this button.

Menu bar:

Basic menus – such as **File**, **Format**, **Edit**, **Tools** and **Help** – and those specific to the program you are using are all available here. When you click the labelled menu button, a small range of options is made available. If you click the double arrows at the end of the list, or rest your mouse on the open menu for a few seconds, you will see the full list of options (see Figure 1.7).

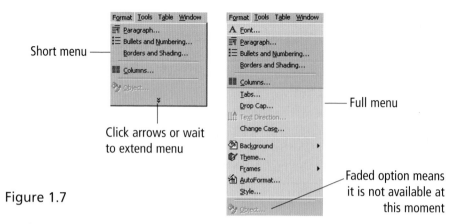

Short menu ———

Click arrows or wait
to extend menu

——— Full menu

Faded option means
it is not available at
this moment

Figure 1.7

Toolbars:

These contain rows of buttons that act as shortcuts to the more common activities carried out when using your computer. Each toolbar has a set of buttons related to a particular group of tasks – for example the drawing toolbar offers you shortcuts to drawing lines or colouring shapes. Toolbar buttons display small pictures indicating the task they perform, but if you forget what they do you can rest your mouse over the button and a definition will appear.

If you need extra toolbar buttons on screen, you can find them by clicking the *More Buttons* arrow. You can add any toolbar from those available via the *View – Toolbars* menu, and add extra buttons permanently by selecting *Customise*.

Scroll bars:

Click the arrows to move horizontally across or vertically up and down the page, or drag the grey box in the appropriate direction.

Status bar:

This provides information such as page numbers, cursor position, print or save status etc.

Taskbar:

This houses the **Start** menu that is always available; any open programs or files that have been minimised; shortcuts (eg to the Desktop or Internet); and useful information (eg date and time etc). *Right*-click to select different ways to arrange several open windows on screen at the same time.

Chapter 2

Organising your work

Once you start to use a computer, you'll soon find that you produce a large number of different files. Locating one again quickly can become quite difficult unless you store them systematically. This chapter looks at how you can manage your computer files successfully. It focuses in particular on:

- Filing on the Desktop
- File management with Windows Explorer
- Moving several files together
- Creating new folders
- Finding missing files
- Creating a shortcut

Filing on the Desktop

Computer file management works on exactly the same principles as office or home filing. Instead of throwing all your correspondence into a single drawer, you probably have drop-files or special folders, labelled *insurance, car, tax, health,* etc, to hold certificates, letters and other relevant documents. In the same way, rather than saving every file directly into the single **My Documents** folder, you need to set up individual, labelled folders where your work can be stored safely. (Later in this book you will see that folders are also used to store favourite Web page addresses (see Chapter 7) and organise your emails (see Chapter 9).)

If you double-click (or select and press Enter) to open the My Computer icon 🖳 , various parts of your computer will be displayed in a window (see Figure 2.1). Double-click the hard disk icon (C:) and you will see a number of folders, including **My Documents**. Inside will be any files you have saved so far.

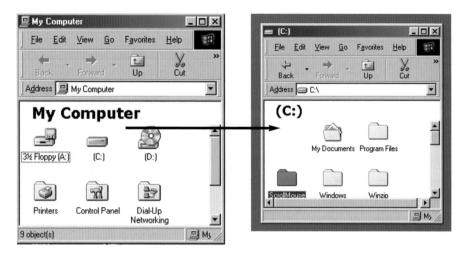

Figure 2.1

To create a new folder inside **My Documents** to hold files you produce relating to insurance matters for example, double-click to open **My Documents**. Then go to File – New – Folder (see Figure 2.2).

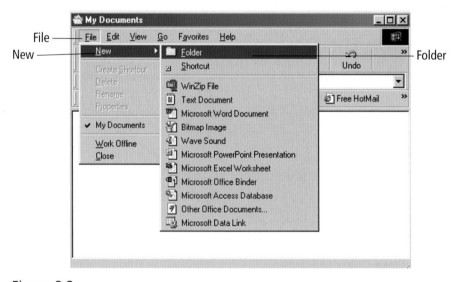

Figure 2.2

A new yellow folder will appear with the temporary name *New Folder* showing over a blue background in a naming box ⬜New Folder .

Anything you type will automatically replace this blue selected text, so type *Insurance* and then press Enter. (If you make a mistake, *right*-click the folder, select **Rename** by clicking this menu option with the left mouse button and try again.) You can make other folders, such as *Health* or *Personal*, in the same way (see Figure 2.3).

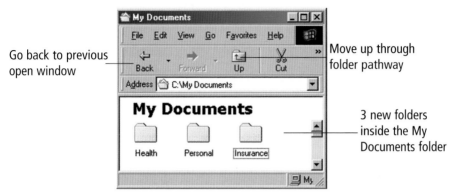

Go back to previous open window

Move up through folder pathway

3 new folders inside the My Documents folder

Figure 2.3

Once you have created a folder in which to place all your insurance-related files, you can sub-divide the folder even further by creating sub-folders. These could then each contain files relating to one aspect of insurance such as *House details*, *Car details,* etc. To do this, first select the 'parent' insurance folder and then go to **File – New – Folder**. The new sub-folder that appears will be *inside* the main folder and the folders structure on your computer will look like Figure 2.4.

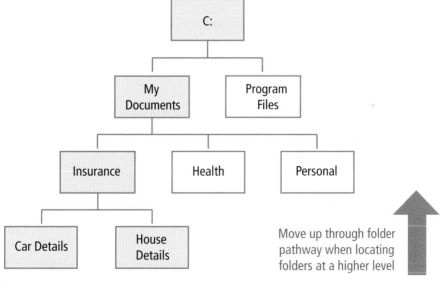

Move up through folder pathway when locating folders at a higher level

Figure 2.4

Once you have created some folders, you can move your files into them (or make copies to place there) very easily. Click on a file (eg *Car insurance*) and drag it across to the folder (see Figure 2.5). When this destination folder turns blue, let go of the mouse and the file will disappear inside. To copy the file but leave the original in place, hold down the Ctrl key on your keyboard as you drag.

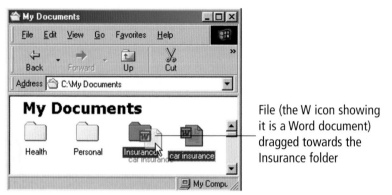

File (the W icon showing it is a Word document) dragged towards the Insurance folder

Figure 2.5

If you drag the selected file holding down the *right* mouse button, a menu appears when you let go offering you the choice of copying or moving the file or cancelling the operation, so there is less chance of a mistake.

If you want to move a file between subfolders and folders, you won't see different levels of folder in the window at the same time and won't be able to drag files between them on screen. Instead, you need to carry out the move in three stages:

1 Select the file and click *Cut* (to move it) or *Copy* (to copy it). It will be placed in part of the computer memory called the Clipboard.
2 Now look in subfolders or go up one or more levels until you can open the destination folder.
3 Click *Paste* and the file will appear inside the window of the open folder.

(In some versions, you can *right*-click the file and choose **Move to** or **Copy to**, select the new destination folder and click *OK*.)

Deleting files or folders is simple – just select them and press the Delete key, remembering to move out any files you want to keep before deleting a folder.

Files that are deleted are actually moved to a different folder – the Recycle Bin – and are only removed permanently when this is emptied. Do this by opening the Bin on the Desktop, or selecting it in Windows Explorer, and going to File – Empty Recycle Bin. Be careful, however, as this option is not available for files on floppy disks; files are permanently removed with immediate effect if you delete any stored here.

File management with Windows Explorer

An alternative way to manage files is to open the file management program, Windows Explorer, from the Start – Programs menu. You will be offered a window divided into two panes – on the left is the folders-only structure and on the right the first level of contents of any selected folder, including any subfolders and files (see Figure 2.6).

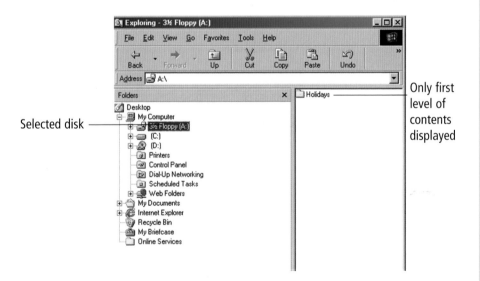

Figure 2.6

If you had saved some files onto a floppy disk and wanted to create folders for them, select 3½" Floppy (A:); otherwise, click (C:). You may need to click the + next to the drive to expand the folders/subfolders structure and display **My Documents** for example. (To contract the structure, click the –.)

To create a new folder, select the 'parent' disk or folder in the left pane and go to **File – New – Folder**.

You can now move or copy files into folders by selecting them and then dragging them across from the right to left panes. Once the destination folder turns blue, let go of the mouse to add your file. If you drag with the *right* mouse button, you open a menu of options (see Figure 2.7).

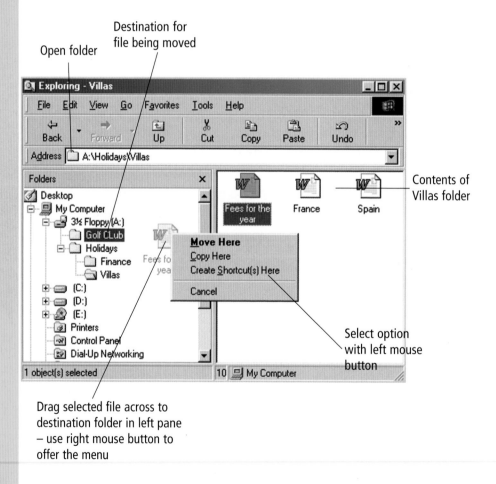

Open folder

Destination for file being moved

Contents of Villas folder

Select option with left mouse button

Drag selected file across to destination folder in left pane – use right mouse button to offer the menu

Figure 2.7

Moving several files together

For a major reorganisation, you may have several files to move across. Instead of dragging them one at a time, you can select either a range of files or non-adjacent files so that, when you drag one, you will move them all together. (It may help if the files are arranged as a list rather than as large icons – if you want to change the arrangement go to View – List.)

Selecting a range of files

1 Click the first in the range.
2 Hold down the Shift key.
3 Click the last in the range – all files between first and last will be selected.
4 Drag one across and they will move together.

Selecting non-adjacent files

1 Click to select the first file.
2 Hold down the Ctrl key.
3 Click other, individual files – all will remain selected.

Creating new folders as they are needed

Within any of the main applications, such as Word, Excel or PowerPoint, you may decide that a current piece of work should be placed in a folder that has not yet been created. Instead of opening Windows Explorer or returning to the Desktop, you can create a folder at the same time as you save your work.

When you click the Save button, you will open the Save As box where you decide on the name and location for your file. If you now click the *Create New Folder* button, you will be able to name a new folder. Click OK and double-click to open it so that it appears in the Save In box. Now when you name your work and click Save, the file will be saved directly into your new folder (see Figure 2.8).

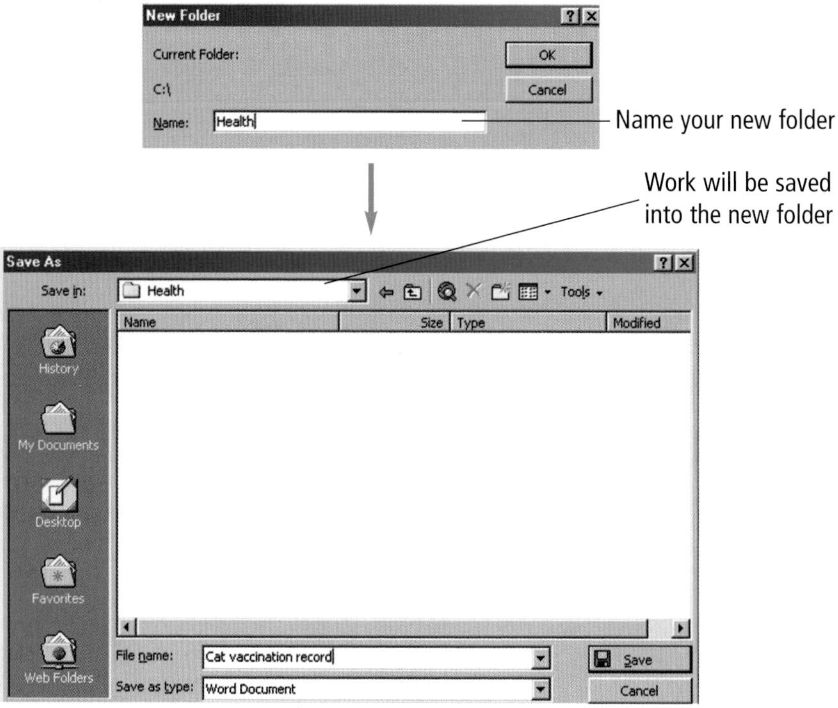

Figure 2.8

Finding missing files

However good your filing system, there will always be files, folders or programs that you cannot find. Fortunately, Windows has an excellent searching facility that you can use.

Files have different extensions at the end of the name (as well as displaying a different icon) depending on which application was used to create them. Here are some of the common file types:

.doc – Word document
.dot – Word template
.xls – Excel workbook
.ppt – PowerPoint
.html – Web page
.txt – Text file
.bmp – Bitmap image file
.jpg – JPEG image file

To locate a file (or folder), select Start – Find or open Windows Explorer and select Tools – Find – Files or Folders. This will open the Find dialog box where you should enter as much information as you can about the file or program.

Make sure that the *Look In* box contains the correct folder location (eg My Documents) or a new one (eg *Holidays*), which you can search for by clicking in the box or using the *Browse* button. If you have no clue where the file was stored, select the correct drive, for example (C:) to look on your hard disk or 3½" Floppy (A:) if you are searching a floppy disk.

Now enter the full folder or filename and any extension – for example *Clip Art* (folder name) or *my letterhead.doc* (file name).

If you only know part of the name, use * for the missing characters – for example *my let*.doc* or **head.doc* or **letter*.** (If you only know some of the words in the name, you can enter these in the *Containing text* box instead, but this is a much slower search.)

To find all files of a particular file type, enter *. (extension) – for example **.bmp*

You can even find a file of unknown name if you have a rough idea of when you saved it. Just click the Date tab and restrict the search to files created between certain dates (see Figure 2.9).

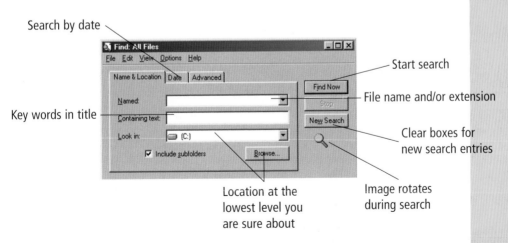

Search by date

Start search

File name and/or extension

Key words in title

Clear boxes for
new search entries

Location at the
lowest level you
are sure about

Image rotates
during search

Figure 2.9

21

Click Find Now and any relevant files will appear in a window underneath the Find dialog box (see Figure 2.10).

Once the search has ended, scroll through the list until you find the file or folder you were looking for. You can either open it directly by double-clicking, or make a note of its specific location for future reference.

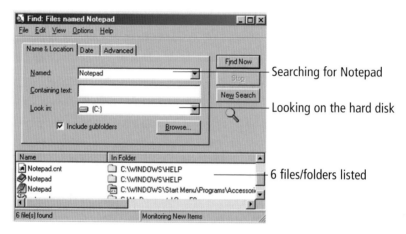

Figure 2.10

Creating a shortcut

If you regularly want to refer to a particular file, or run a program that is buried deep amongst your computer files, you can create a shortcut to it via the Desktop.

One method is to find the file from My Computer or Windows Explorer and *right*-click to give you the option to Send to – Desktop (create shortcut). You can also start on an empty part of the Desktop, *right*-click and select New – Shortcut. Browse through your program files until you find your target. Click Open to place the filename in the box, Next for your own choice of name and then OK to create the shortcut.

Shortcuts created on the Desktop normally show a small arrow, and you can change the name if you want to by clicking the name box once, or by *right*-clicking and selecting *Rename*.

Chapter 3

Word processing

Even if you are a slow typist, word processing has many advantages:

- Documents are far easier to read than handwritten material.
- Copies of all your work are simple to save on disk.
- Making changes no longer requires typing everything again.
- It looks far more professional for business or official documents.
- There are a wide range of special effects you can incorporate into your work.
- If you use email, you can attach word-processed documents to your messages and send them at the same time.

There are numerous books devoted to Microsoft Word as well as the other main software applications, and you may want to look at one of these for a detailed introduction to word processing. However, this chapter outlines the basic steps you can take to get started. There is also a labelled keyboard picture on page 27, and checklist at the end of the chapter, that you can refer to whenever you need to remind yourself where things are or how to do something.

The chapter looks in detail at:

- Creating a document
- Letters
- Autotext
- Templates
- Dates
- Working with pictures
- Mail merge

Creating a document

When you open Microsoft Word, you are presented with a blank screen – 'a clean sheet of paper' – and can start typing straightaway. The text will appear at the position marked by the cursor, which appears a short way in from the top left-hand corner of the screen to leave space for the top and left margins.

Using the same techniques as in typewriting (eg holding down the Shift key to produce a capital letter or symbol at the top of a key, or pressing the Space bar between words), you will be able to start creating your first document. You will notice that the computer 'wraps' the text down the page for you, so that you don't need to take any action to start typing on a new line when you reach the right-hand margin of the page.

Editing

To move the flashing black cursor to a different position, you click the mouse pointer on screen when it shows a thin vertical bar.

Alternatively, you can press the cursor (also called 'arrow') key on your keyboard that points in the appropriate direction. You can then correct mistakes or add extra words.

Delete incorrect letters next to the cursor with the Backspace key (erasing to the left) or Delete key (erasing to the right). When you type your new letters they will be inserted in the space.

To start a new paragraph, you need to press the Enter key (sometimes called the Return key) to move the cursor to the beginning of a new line, and you can keep pressing it if you want a larger gap before typing again. As it takes any text to its *right* down the page with it, you will need to ensure first of all that the cursor is at the end of your text. Otherwise you can easily split words or sentences. (If you do this by mistake, pressing the Backspace key will join your words up again by deleting the space you made.)

Saving

So that you won't lose your work because of a mistake or any technical problems, it is always a good idea to save your new document early, and then update it regularly as you make further changes.

On clicking the **Save** toolbar button ![save icon] you will open a **Save As** dialog box and need to specify where you want to save your work (eg into the My Documents folder or onto a floppy disk) and what recognisable name to give it (see Figure 3.1). Once you have checked or amended the information in the **Save In** and **File name** boxes, press the Enter key or click the **Save** button and your work will be saved. You will see that the Title bar across the top of your screen will now display the file's new name rather than the temporary title *Document 1*. Once saved and named, clicking the **Save** button will update the document automatically.

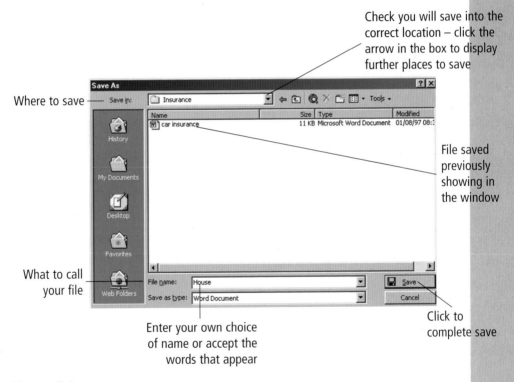

Check you will save into the correct location – click the arrow in the box to display further places to save

Where to save

File saved previously showing in the window

What to call your file

Click to complete save

Enter your own choice of name or accept the words that appear

Figure 3.1

Changing the look of your document

The appearance of your document (its 'format') depends on the formatting settings pre-defined within Word that are known as the 'default' settings. To underline a heading, or increase the size of your text, for example, you will need to change the settings. This can be carried out before you start typing, or you can select particular words or sections of text and then apply new formatting just to this selection.

There are various ways to select words or blocks of text, using either mouse or keyboard, and these are set out in the checklist at the end of the chapter. Selected text will always appear as white letters on a black background (you may have noticed this happening by mistake as you created your document) and you can take off the selection by clicking the mouse button anywhere else on screen away from the left margin.

Once you have selected some words, you can use the toolbar buttons to change them to **Bold** **B** , *Italic* *I* , Underlined **U** or coloured **A** and alter the size or type of character (font) from the drop-down lists available. Many boxes on screen have a small downward-facing arrow next to them – click the arrow to display a list of alternative choices you can make.

Alternatively, you can open the Format – Font dialog box and preview the changes to your selected text before accepting them by clicking OK.

To revert to the default settings, you may need to click the toolbar buttons off again before continuing your typing.

Selected paragraphs can also be changed so that, for example, text is centred on the page or line spacing is doubled. If choices aren't available as toolbar buttons, open the Format – Paragraph dialog box to select and preview alternatives. (If carrying on typing, don't forget to press the Enter key and change the settings if you want to revert back to an earlier alignment or spacing option.)

In this way you can change the appearance of your documents to an enormous extent with just a couple of clicks of the mouse.

Printing

When you are happy with your document, and as long as a suitable printer has been installed correctly, is turned on and has paper in it, you can print a single copy by clicking the Print toolbar button .

Main keys on the keyboard

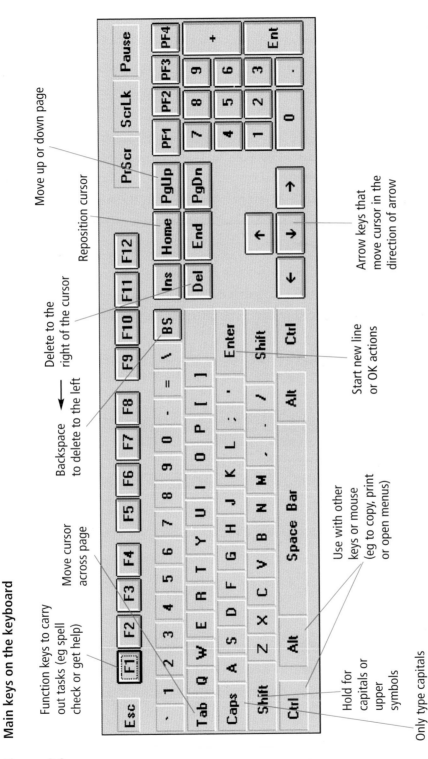

Function keys to carry
out tasks (eg spell
check or get help)

Move cursor
across page

Delete to the
right of the cursor

Backspace
to delete to the left

Move up or down page

Reposition cursor

Arrow keys that
move cursor in the
direction of arrow

Start new line
or OK actions

Use with other
keys or mouse
(eg to copy, print
or open menus)

Hold for
capitals or
upper
symbols

Only type capitals

Figure 3.2

For a range of options such as printing several copies, printing onto different sizes of paper or printing selected pages of a long document, you will need to select options in the **Print** or **Page Setup** dialog boxes opened via the **File** menu.

Letters

Writing official letters can be a chore. Fortunately, there are a number of useful features in Word to make the job easier. If you play a role in a local society, association or charity, for example, these shortcuts can help you save a great deal of time and effort when carrying out your administrative tasks. You can:

- use shortcuts to enter commonly used words or dates automatically;
- create templates to use over and over again;
- save time when sending the same letter to everyone on a mailing list; and
- make them look more attractive by inserting pictures from a ready-made gallery.

Layout

Word-processed letters follow the same rules as those applied when writing by hand. People often save time by leaving out the commas after each line of an address and by setting everything down the left margin (ie left aligned).

A typical letter that might be sent out by the secretary of a local association enclosing the annual programme of events is shown on the next page (Figure 3.3).

AutoText

One way to save time is to store common text such as an address (which could even include a picture as part of a logo) as *AutoText*. This can then be inserted automatically into any document with a few keystrokes.

Hambledean Allotment Association

Greys Road

Stoke

ST5 7RG

Mr. P. White

25 Abbey Way

Stoke

ST5 2LR

29 June 2001

Dear Peter

Please find enclosed a copy of this year's calendar of events. I think you'll agree that the committee has put together a very interesting programme.

Do look through and let me know which talks you would like to attend, so that I can arrange suitable refreshments.

I look forward to seeing you at the summer garden party.

Yours sincerely

Mavis Applewood

Secretary

Figure 3.3

Set out the address as you want it to appear in your documents and then select the entire block of text. Now select the Insert – AutoText – New menu option and in the *Name* box type in a few letters or a short word to identify the selection – eg *haa* (short for Hambledean Allotment Association). Then click OK.

Next time you want to insert the address into your letter, type haa and then press the function key F3 that you will find at the top of your keyboard. The address will appear.

Templates

To reproduce a complete layout that could include your address and some text in your chosen font, together with your letter ending, you may prefer to create a *template*, so that you can use this every time you type a similar letter. The template is kept with others in a templates folder and remains unchanged when you use it to create your documents. (See Chapter 2 for more information on folders.)

Open Word, or start a new, blank document, and type as much of your letter as you will want to save and use repeatedly. Then click the Save button to open the *Save As* window.

To save a template rather than normal Word document, select *Document Template* from the drop-down list in the Save As Type box (see Figure 3.4).

Once you do this, you will see that the Save In box shows the Template folders and, if you want to save your letter in a particular sub-folder, select it in the window and open it so that it shows in the Save In box. Name the file (eg *H-address)* and click Save.

If you prefer, create and name a new folder to hold groups of related templates by first clicking the *Create New Folder* button.

To use the template in future, go to File – New and click the correct tab (eg *Letters and Faxes, Publications, Letterheads* etc) to locate your template. Select the template from those showing in the window and, with the *Create New Document* option chosen, click OK (Figure 3.5).

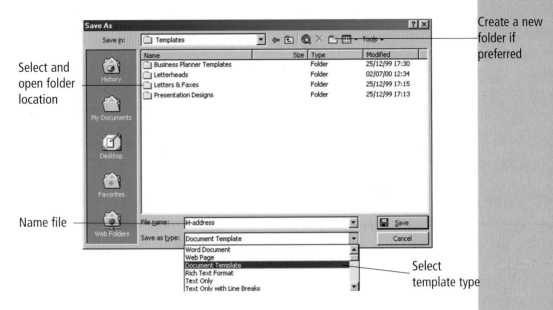

Create a new folder if preferred

Select and open folder location

Name file

Select template type

Figure 3.4

Your basic letter layout will appear and you can now continue to write and save your letter in the normal way.

You can use the same method to create templates for a range of documents that you produce regularly, such as headed notepaper, invitations, programmes, newsletters, reports or minutes of meetings.

Select template   Click correct tab

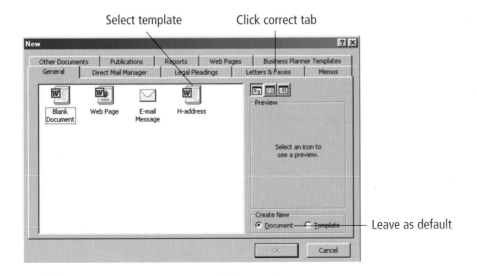

Leave as default

Figure 3.5

To save even more time, go to **File – New** and check the Template tabs first to see if the proposed document already exists as a template. Then, if you want to create your own customised version, you can select the option *Create New Template* when you open the original. After making changes to suit your own needs, save the amended template (temporarily titled Template1) with a different name.

Dates

Word can put in today's date for you with a few mouse clicks. Position the cursor where you want the date to appear and select **Insert – Date and Time** to open the dialog box (see Figure 3.6). Select your preferred style of date and then click **OK** to return to your document. If you will be delaying printing but want that day's date in your document, click the *Update* box.

To save time in future, click the *Default* button when you first select a style of date so that your preferred format is always selected every time you open the **Date and Time** dialog box.

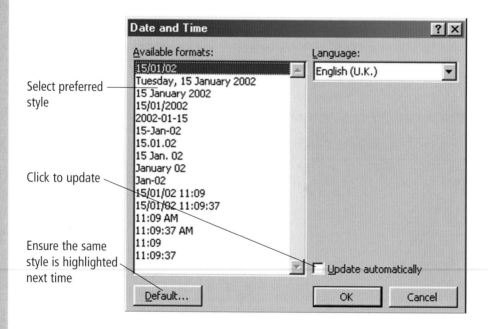

Select preferred style

Click to update

Ensure the same style is highlighted next time

Figure 3.6

Working with pictures

To enhance the appearance of your stationery, you may like to include a picture that can then either be saved with a template or simply inserted each time you write a letter by adding it to your AutoText list.

You can choose to use pictures available in the ready-made Clip Art Gallery installed with Word, or from a CD-ROM, or from file (ie insert an image that has previously been saved on disk). Once it appears on the page, you can resize or reposition it or carry out more detailed editing using the Picture toolbar.

Inserting Clip Art

To open up the gallery, click the **Insert Clip Art** toolbar button 🔳 on the Drawing toolbar, or go to **Insert – Picture – Clip Art**. (To display the toolbar, either click the **Drawing** button 🔳 or go to **View – Toolbars – Drawing**.)

Select any category and scroll down through the pictures until you find one that you like. You could also type in a subject in the search box to display all relevant pictures (see Figure 3.7). Press the Enter key to begin the search.

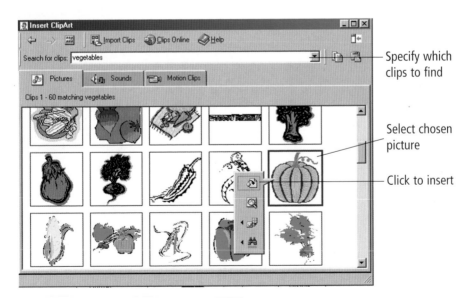

Figure 3.7a

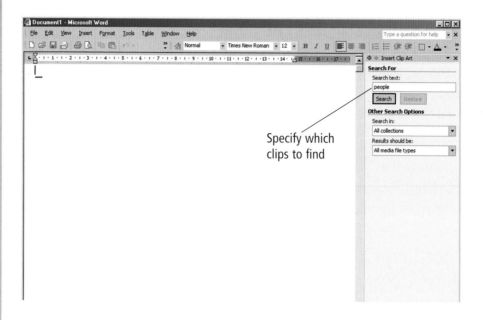

Specify which
clips to find

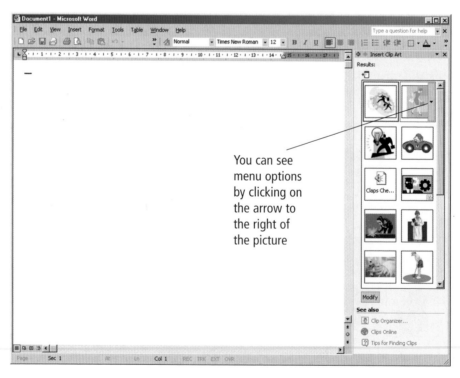

You can see
menu options
by clicking on
the arrow to
the right of
the picture

Figure 3.7b Using the **Insert – Picture – Clip Art** menu in Word 2002
brings up a screen like the one at the top. Once you select a category
of Clip Art you will see a screen like that at the bottom

Click once to select your chosen picture and then click the Insert clip button 🔁 that appears. Close the gallery to reveal your picture.

After first *selecting* the picture by clicking it to show a black border, you can amend it in one of the following three ways:

- If you change your mind and don't like it after all, just press the Delete key. You can now return to the gallery and find another picture.
- To change its size, move the mouse pointer over any little black box (referred to as a 'sizing handle') visible on the border and, when it shows a two-way arrow, gently click and drag the border in or out.
- Finally, use the normal Word alignment buttons to centre the picture or realign it to the left or right of the page.

Moving pictures around

You may want to have more control over the siting of a picture than is allowed by the alignment settings, and to do this you can insert it into a 'Text Box'. This box, with the picture inside, can then be dragged round the screen to any position.

Click the Text Box button 📄 on the Drawing toolbar and then either click on screen or click and drag to create a box. The mouse pointer will show a small cross and a flashing cursor will appear inside the box.

Now insert a Clip Art picture as normal. This will be inserted *inside* the Text Box. (You can also select a picture that has already been inserted and then click the Text Box button to site it in the box, but you may then need to resize the picture to centre it correctly.)

Move the mouse pointer over the Text Box and, when it shows a four-way arrow, you will be able to click and drag it across the screen. You can also resize either Text Box or picture by dragging one of the borders with the two-way arrow over a sizing handle.

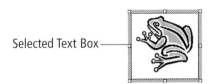

Selected Text Box

Figure 3.8

To remove the visible Text Box border, select it to show its thick edge and *white* sizing handles and then select *No Line* from the Line Colour palette (see Figure 3.9). Alternatively, emphasise the border using the line options available.

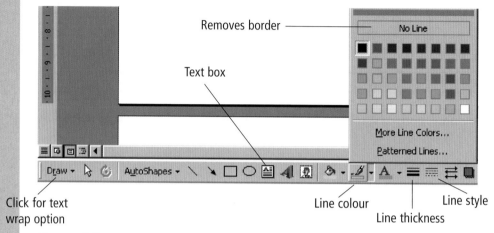

Removes border — No Line

Text box

More Line Colors...
Patterned Lines...

Draw ▾   AutoShapes ▾

Click for text wrap option

Line colour   Line style
Line thickness

Figure 3.9

Another way of dragging a picture is to select it and then click *Draw – Text Wrapping* on the Drawing toolbar. This option sets the way that text will wrap round a picture inserted in a document. After choosing a style such as *Tight*, you will find that the black sizing handles now appear white and you can drag the picture round the screen.

Editing a picture

For more detailed changes, you need to *right*-click the picture to reveal a menu of options (Figure 3.10). You can then choose some of the following:

From the Picture toolbar

Image control: create a black and white or greyscale image or fade it into the background as a watermark.

Contrast or *Brightness*: click these up or down.

Crop: cut off a section of the picture by clicking the button and then dragging in the picture border over a sizing handle when the mouse pointer shows the cropping symbol.

Text wrap: choose how the text on the page will wrap round your picture.

Reset: click if you have made too many changes and want to start again.

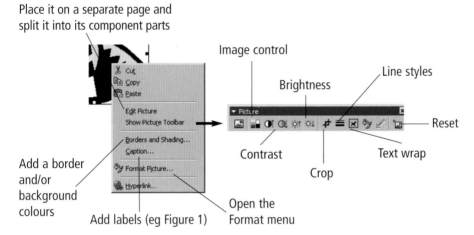

Figure 3.10

Pictures from elsewhere

Having a scanner or digital camera allows you to create and save a range of photos or drawings that can then be inserted into your word-processed documents. Alternatively, you can borrow or buy a CD-ROM full of images you can use.

To insert an image into an open document, minimise the document (see page 11) and then select and open the picture. Click the *Copy* toolbar button, restore your Word document from the taskbar, click in place with the cursor and then click *Paste*. (You can also insert a picture by locating it after clicking Insert – Picture – From File and clicking the Insert button or pressing Enter.)

If you find a picture on the Web that you'd like to store for future use (as long as it won't infringe any copyright), it is a very simple process to save this onto your computer. *Right*-click the mouse on the image and, from the short menu that appears, select *Save Picture As*. This will then open the normal Save As window and you can name and save the picture into an appropriate folder.

Mail merge

Mail merge is used when sending the same letter to large numbers of people. It allows you to write *one* letter (the 'Main Document') and then insert individual names and addresses drawn from a separately created mailing list (the 'Data Source'). You could use Word or an application such as Excel (spreadsheet) to create the Data Source (for further information on databases, see pages 105–107).

The Main Document

If you look at the example of a letter on page 29, you will see that only a few entries are personal:

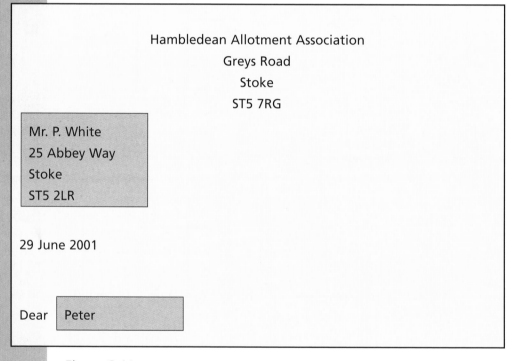

Hambledean Allotment Association
Greys Road
Stoke
ST5 7RG

Mr. P. White
25 Abbey Way
Stoke
ST5 2LR

29 June 2001

Dear   Peter

Figure 3.11

For a mail merge operation, you would probably open a new, blank Word document (or saved letter template) in readiness, but you could use any document previously created, as long as you remove the personal details it contained.

To start the process and produce a similar letter, go to **Tools** – Mail Merge and in the box that appears click 1. *Main Document* – *Create*. You must select *Form Letters* for any type of mailing unless you want to create envelopes or labels, and *Active Window* to use the document open on screen (Figure 3.12).

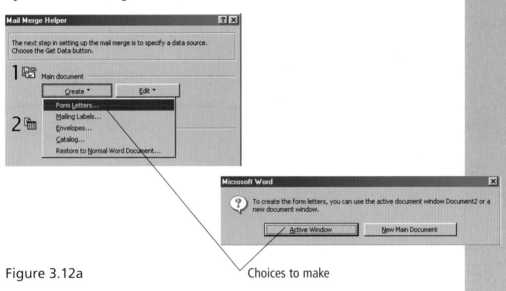

Figure 3.12a   Choices to make

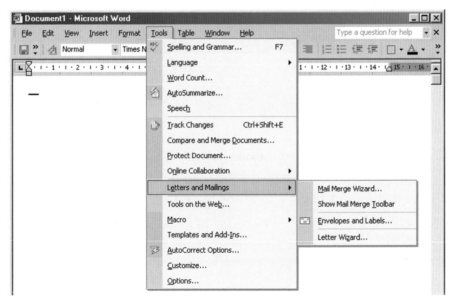

Figure 3.12b In Word 2002, if you select *Tools – Letters and Mailings – Mail Merge Wizard*, you will be helped through the mail merge operation

The Data Source

Now you need to create the mailing list of names and addresses.

Click 2. *Data Source – Get Data* in the mail merge helper dialog box and then select *Create Data Source*.

To use the database for a range of purposes in the future, include as many categories (field names) as you can (eg *FirstName, Surname, Initials, Title, PhoneNumber*, etc) even if they won't all be used for this particular letter. Some appropriate field names will be offered to you, but you may need to create some of your own and delete others you will never want to use (see Figure 3.13). Field names should not include any spaces or punctuation.

Enter new
field name
and click Add
button

Select
unwanted field
name and click
Remove button

Click to save
database field
name list

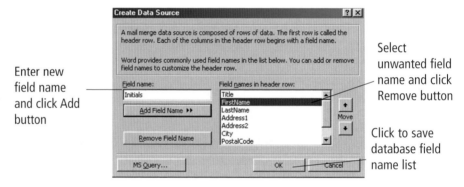

Figure 3.13

Click **OK** and save the Data Source under a suitable name (eg *HAAmembers*).

To add everyone's details to the database, click *Edit Data Source*. You can now start typing in the first record – in the example this is Peter White's name and address – in the boxes provided on the Data Form (see Figure 3.14). When a record is complete, click *Add New* to add the next person's details, and only click **OK** when all the names and addresses have been typed in (or you've entered as many as you want to in a session).

To return to the Data Form at any time to add new details, click the *Edit Data Source* toolbar button ▥ on the Mail Merge toolbar that will be visible in your main document. (If not visible, open this via the

View – **Toolbars** menu.) You could also open the data source file (eg *HAAmembers*) where the records will be displayed as a table.

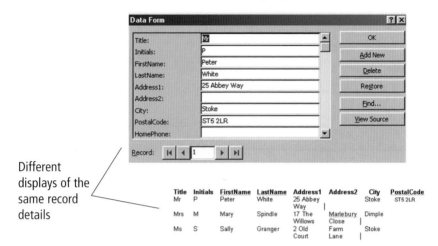

Different
displays of the
same record
details

Figure 3.14

Merging the data

After clicking **OK** you will return to your main document. The Mail Merge toolbar will appear and it includes an **Insert Merge Field** button. As you start typing your letter, click the button and select an appropriate field name wherever personal details need to be included (see Figure 3.15). The field names will appear within <<chevrons>> against a grey background as they are 'fields' and will be replaced by data drawn from the database when your records and letter are merged.

Check the finished appearance of the letters by clicking the <<ABC>> **View Merged Data** button, and make any necessary adjustments, for example to spacing.

Printing

If you are ready to print straightaway, click the **Merge to Printer** button . Otherwise, close and save both the Main Document and the records you have added to the Data Source file. When you open the Main Document again in the future, the database will be linked automatically and you can print your letters then.

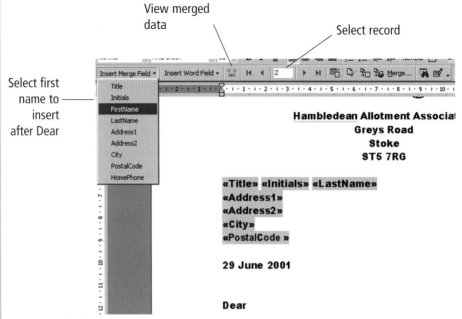

Figure 3.15

If you ever take your letters to another machine to print, and so could leave the Data Source file behind, you should click **Merge to New Document** instead. This creates a new file in which each letter contains details from one record and is laid out to print on a new page.

Finally, if you wanted to send selected letters out – for example just to those members living in Stoke – you should go to **Tools – Mail Merge** and select *3. Query options*. Select the Field name (eg *Town*) and the criteria (eg *equal to*) and then type *Stoke* before clicking **OK**. Back in the **Mail Merge** dialog box, click *Merge* and then choose to print directly or save to file.

Labels

Once you have printed all your letters, it can save time if you create labels automatically. This is very easy to do using the mail merge facility as you can base them on the Data Source that you have already saved.

Click **Tools – Mail Merge** and select *Main Document – Create – Mailing Labels*. You then need to open the Data Source file you saved (*Data Source – Get Data*) and then go on to *Set up the Main Document*.

After choosing appropriately sized label paper (which you can buy in most good stationers), click **OK** to open the *Create Labels* dialog box (see Figure 3.16).

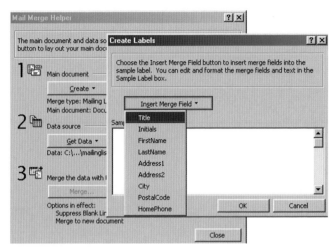

Figure 3.16

For every field you must select the appropriate field name from the *Insert Merge Field* list, and space the field names as they should appear in a label using the Space bar or Enter key. Your labels will then be based on field names arranged as follows:

«Title» «Initials» «LastName»
«Address1»
«Address2»
«City»
«PostalCode»

You can now insert the label paper into the printer and print your labels directly or save them as a *New Document* to print later.

Labels can be useful not just for mail merge, but also for other purposes, such as for dinner party place names, your return address on parcels, storage boxes or jars of home-made jam. You can create them directly by selecting **Tools – Envelopes and Labels**. Click *Options* to select the correct size of label sheets on which to print.

43

To produce different labels on the same sheet, click *New Document* and type your text into the various label outlines. If the outlines are not visible, select the **Table – Show Gridlines** option.

You can produce a sheet of identical labels by entering the text into the Address window (see Figure 3.17).

Click **Print** to print the labels straightaway or view them by clicking **New Document** and save them to print another time.

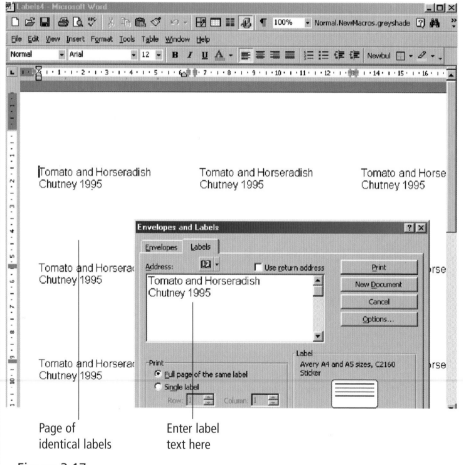

Figure 3.17

Checklist

Checklist of the basic word-processing operations in Word

Launch Word	Go to *Start – Programs – Microsoft Word* or double-click the Word icon showing on the Desktop.
Start a new document	Click the New button .
Open a named, saved document	■ Click the Open button . ■ If necessary, click in the Look In box to find the correct drive, or open folders showing in the window until you find the location of the file. ■ Select it and click Open or press the Enter key.
Check one spelling or grammatical mistake	Right-click any word underlined in red or green, and select an alternative word from the list.
Check the whole document	■ Click the Spelling button to open the dialog box. ■ Select an alternative spelling, or manually alter spelling or grammar, then click *Change* to amend your document. ■ Continue checking or click the Cancel button.
Enter text	■ Hold down the Shift key to type a capital letter or punctuation at the top of a key (eg * or %) ■ The apostrophe ' is the *lower* symbol under @. ■ Press Caps Lock before entering a line of text in capitals, and press it off before continuing. ■ Press the tab key to move the cursor across the page in jumps of 0.5" or 1.27 cm.

	■ Press Enter only when you want to start a new paragraph. Otherwise, leave 'word-wrap' to move text in long sentences automatically onto the next line.
Amend entries	Use the Backspace key (← above the Enter key) to delete to the left of the cursor, and the Delete key to delete to the right.
Correct mistakes	Click the Undo button ↰ repeatedly to step back through your actions.
Cancel overtyping	If entries start replacing text, press the Insert key or double-click the letters OVR showing in the Status bar. This returns you to Insert mode.
Move round the document	■ Click the mouse to position the cursor where you want to type. ■ Press Home to move to the start of a line. ■ Press End to move to the end of a line. ■ Hold Ctrl as you press Home/End to move to the start/end of the whole document. ■ Click the arrow keys in the appropriate direction to move the cursor through the text. ■ Drag the grey box or click the arrows in the vertical or horizontal scroll bar to move up or down the page. ■ Press Page Up or Page Down to move through large blocks of text.

Get help	■ From the *Help – Microsoft Word Help* menu or after clicking the Help button ⟨?⟩, select *Contents* for a topic list, *Answer Wizard* to type a question and *Index* to search for keywords.
	■ Choose *Show Office Assistant* or press key F1 to introduce the Clippit helper.
	■ Choose *What's This?* and click part of the window to see a definition.
Select (highlight) text	■ Double-click a word.
	■ Click and drag the mouse across an entry.
	■ Hold down the Shift key and then press an arrow key in the relevant direction.
	■ Click to place the cursor at the start of a section, use the scroll bar to move to the end of the section and hold the Shift key as you click the mouse again.
	■ When the pointer in the left margin shows a right-facing arrow, click to select the line or click and drag to select several.
	■ Hold Ctrl and press the letter A to select the whole document, or go to *Edit – Select All*.
Take off a highlight	Click the mouse anywhere in the document – do *not* press a key on the keyboard or you will delete the text.

Format (change) text	■ After it has been highlighted, use the toolbar buttons to change to **B**old, *I*talic, <u>Underline</u>, or the size or type of font. ■ Go to *Format – Font* for special effects or to preview changes.
Alter line spacing	■ Select the paragraph and then press Ctrl plus 2 to double-space, Ctrl plus 1 to single space, and Ctrl plus 5 for 1.5 spacing. ■ Open the *Format – Paragraph* dialog box to select specific measurements.
Align text (position on the page)	Use the alignment buttons to Left align, Centre, Right align or Justify (spread text evenly across the page).
Indent paragraphs	■ Select text and use the Decrease or Increase Indent buttons to move the left indent in or out. ■ Open the *Format – Paragraph* dialog box to set left or right indents in exact units.
Copy formatting	■ Select an example of the formatted text, click the Format Painter button and then highlight the text you wish to change – the pointer will now show a paintbrush. ■ Select text to change and apply a new set of font/paragraph instructions from the drop-down list in the Style box.

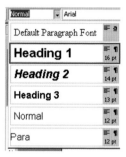

Move or copy text by dragging	■ Select text to move.
	■ Move pointer over selected block until you see a white, left-facing arrow.
	■ Click and hold down mouse button. A box will appear at the end of the arrow.
	■ Drag the arrow to the new position for the text, which will be marked by a dotted vertical line.
	■ Let go of the mouse and the text will drop into place.
	■ To *copy*, hold down Ctrl as you drag. You will see a + sign attached to the arrow.
Move or copy text using Cut or Copy & Paste	■ Select text to move.
	■ Click *Cut* button ✂ or select *Edit – Cut*.
	■ (To *copy* text and leave original in place, click *Copy* button 📋 or select *Edit – Copy*.)
	■ Click in new position for text, placing flashing cursor on screen.
	■ Click *Paste* button 📋 or select *Edit – Paste*.

Save your work for the first time	■ Click the *Save* button 💾 to open the *Save As* dialog box. ■ Choose the appropriate location (ie the folder you want to save it in) from the window or drop-down list in the *Save In* box. ■ Change (by typing over) or accept the entry in the *File Name* box. ■ Click the *Save* button or press Enter.
Update your work	Click the Save button regularly.
Create a new version	Select *File – Save As* to open the *Save As* dialog box, enter an alternative location and/or name and press Enter.
Margins	■ Go to *File – Page Setup – Margins* and change the measurements in the boxes. ■ Move the pointer over the left or right edges of the ruler between the white and grey areas and, when it shows the two-way arrow, click and drag the margin in or out.
Preview your work ready for printing	■ Click the Print Preview button 🔍 and click on the screen to zoom in. ■ If a small amount of text goes over the page, click the *Shrink to Fit* button 📑 to reduce the font size. ■ Click the Close button to return to your document.

Print

■ Click the *Print* button 🖨 to print one copy of the current document on the default (pre-set) printer.

■ Go to *File – Print* if you want to select an alternative printer or change the number of copies/pages to print before clicking OK.

Chapter 4

Publishing using Word

To produce bookmarks, dinner menus, place names, flyers, newspaper advertisements, newsletters or other specialist stationery items, you don't need a separate desktop publishing application as you can use many of the same facilities that are offered by your word processing package. For example, you can display text in columns, add numbers or bullets to list items, border or shade sections of text and insert special features such as WordArt. This chapter looks at how to do this in Word. It looks specifically at:

- Creating a leaflet (including columns, lists and borders and shading)
- Using WordArt
- Drawings
- Tables

Leaflets

When you are designing a leaflet, you need to think about exactly where the text or pictures should be placed. For every A4 piece of paper, you may have sections that are blank, and parts that will be *created* as a new document but *printed* on the reverse of the original, so you must take care when replacing the paper in the printer. You can also customise the page set-up by selecting **Paper size** and choosing differently sized paper on which to print.

Black and white can look very smart, especially if printed onto coloured paper. However, using a colour printer or taking your file on disk into a print shop may be worthwhile if you want the best colour effect or a large number of items produced.

One example of the type of leaflet you could produce is the Hambledean Allotment Association programme (see Figure 4.1), which is a three-fold leaflet based on two A4 documents printed on both sides of a single sheet of paper.

Figure 4.1

For this kind of leaflet, each page needs to be re-orientated from upright ('portrait') to lengthways ('landscape') via the File – Page Set up – Paper size menu option, and then divided into three equal columns (see Figure 4.2). (A less ambitious leaflet could be produced based on two columns with a central fold.)

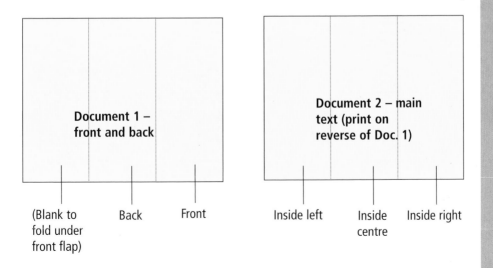

Figure 4.2

Columns of text

You can change to columns *after* entering text if you first select the block of text and then apply the change to the selected section, or you can set up column formatting first of all.

You can also insert pictures or drawings into the columns and decide where each column will break on the page.

For straightforward columns, simply click the **Column** toolbar button ▦ and drag the mouse across to set the number.

To choose which piece of text begins in column 2 or 3, rather than leaving it to wrap round at the bottom of the page, click in front of the first word and select **Insert – Break – Column Break**.

For more options, you need to open the **Columns** dialog box by selecting *Format – Columns* (see Figure 4.3). Here you can amend the column widths by selecting identical or uneven columns, and, if necessary, altering the exact measurements displayed in the Width and Spacing section. You can also add a dividing line and apply the formatting to particular sections of a document. This is important if you want to leave a central heading or earlier text unaltered, as you can select *Apply To: This Point Forward,* or *Selected Text.*

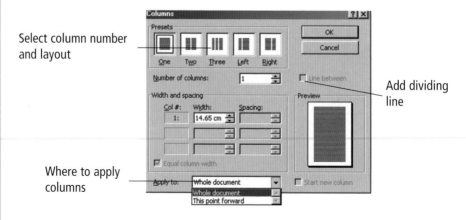

Select column number and layout

Add dividing line

Where to apply columns

Figure 4.3

When you want to return to a normal layout after creating columns, open the Columns dialog box again and select one column: *Apply To This Point Forward*.

For Document 1 (ie the front/back of the Hambledean leaflet) format three columns and then insert a column break straightaway, leaving a blank first column that will fold inside the front page. This moves the cursor to the beginning of column 2, where you need to press the Enter key several times to move down the page. Now you can type in the contact details. These should be aligned centrally and will be visible at the back of the programme.

For something like the Hambledean programme you may prefer to create Document 2, the main programme text, first of all.

Either type it as a normal document and then select the text and apply three columns to your selection, or set the column formatting first and type September–December details in column 1 (see Figure 4.4).

You will need to insert a column break before the February talk, so that the details start at the top of column 2, and again in front of the June trip. You may also need to edit the text or column width, to make sure the columns look roughly equal.

Lists

You will see that the events in the programme are displayed as a bulleted list.

There are two different ways to produce lists:

1 If you type the list without formatting, but place each item on a new line, you can then select all the text and click on the *Numbering* ⅰ☰ or *Bullets* ☰ toolbar buttons.
2 You can click on screen and then click the appropriate toolbar button *before* typing the first item. The first number or bullet will appear automatically and every time you press Enter a new one will be displayed.

- **22 September:** Preparing the Ground. Talk and demonstration of garden tools by staff at the Howbye Garden Centre.
- **18 October:** Quiz Night in the Hambledean Hall.
- **24 November:** Bulbs for Spring. Talk by Harry Spendle.
- **20 December:** Christmas Ball. Music by the *Skinflints*. Prizes presented by the Lord Mayor.

- **18 February:** Getting the Most from your Catalogues. Talk by Martin Potter.
- **27 March:** Visit to the Hawthorne Castle Gardens. Book early to avoid disappoint-ment.
- **24 April:** Hanging Baskets. Demonstration by Serena Hamilton of Global Flowers.
- **17 May:** Fertilisers, Sprays or Organic? Discussion chaired by Fred Peters.

- **29 June:** Trip to the Lake District Conservancy Centre.
- **17 July:** Dahlias. Talk by Gladys Whittle. Bring along diseased plants for her expert advice.
- **15 August:** Garden Party and Root Vegetables competition.
- In the evening, hosting BBC Gardeners' Question Time in the Hambledean Hall. Book early!

Figure 4.4

Choose from a range of number or bullet styles by opening the **Format – Bullets and Numbering** dialog box (Figure 4.5). You can change the spacing between text and bullets/numbers via the *Customize* button, and then click *Bullet* to view the gallery of further styles.

Whenever you want a line *without* a number or bullet, place the cursor in the line and click off the toolbar button. You can also create the same effect by holding the Shift key as you press Enter whilst you are typing the list.

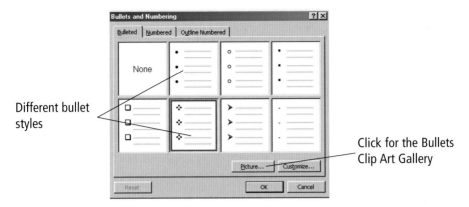

Different bullet styles

Click for the Bullets Clip Art Gallery

Figure 4.5

Borders and shading

You may like to make the text stand out with a border and/or shading. Many different effects are possible using the Format – Borders and Shading menu options (see Figure 4.6). You can select a paragraph or section and add a line surround and/or shade the background (and there are even various lines and styles, including small pictures, that can be used to border a complete page).

Border whole page

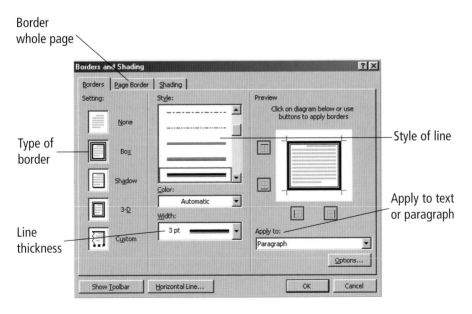

Type of border

Line thickness

Style of line

Apply to text or paragraph

Figure 4.6

To border just the text, select it first and then apply the effects to *text* and not *paragraph*. If you want the border to extend a small way past the text, but not across the complete page, border the paragraph but then indent it both left and right by increasing the measurements in the Format – Paragraph – Indents and Spacing dialog box.

→ | This is an indented paragraph border | ←

This is shading applied to text

a more fancy effect on a full paragraph

To continue typing below bordered text, double click the mouse pointer to place the cursor on the page. (In earlier versions of Word, it is hard to 'get out' of a bordered paragraph. A good tip is to press Enter a few times to clear yourself a space before going back to create the text border.)

Using WordArt

To make your text stand out, instead of simply selecting an unusual font and size, you can insert a text object created in a separate package – Microsoft WordArt. This can be shaped, coloured or stretched and will replace a heading or other normal text.

This is Times New Roman size 14 text

This is Times New Roman WordArt

For the Hambledean programme, insert a further column break and you are ready to add the WordArt title on the front cover of the leaflet in column 3, Document 1.

Click the *WordArt* button 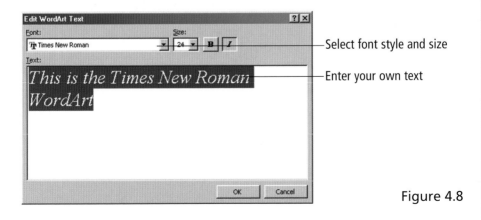 on the Drawing toolbar. From the gallery of styles that appears, select your preferred example (although this can be changed later) and click **OK** (see Figure 4.7).

Select example ——

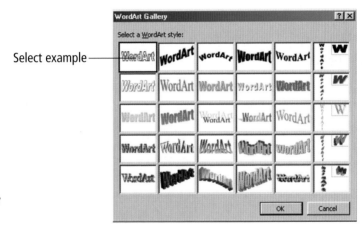

Figure 4.7

You will be taken to the **Edit WordArt Text** window (see Figure 4.8) and can now type in your text.

—Select font style and size

—Enter your own text

Figure 4.8

Make changes to font type and style using the toolbar at the top of the window and then click **OK** to return to your document.

Use the WordArt toolbar that appears to make various changes, such as apply a different colour, re-orientate the text or increase spaces between letters (see Figure 4.9). To go back to the WordArt editing box to alter the text, click the *Edit Text* toolbar button or double-click the WordArt object. To return to the document, click *OK*.

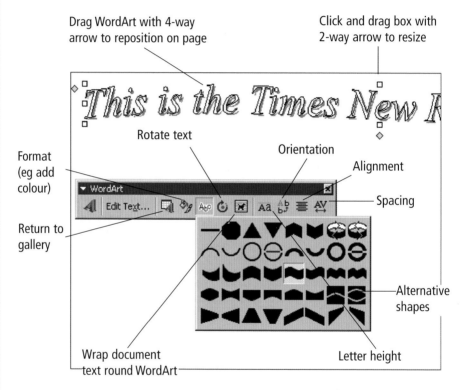

Drag WordArt with 4-way arrow to reposition on page

Click and drag box with 2-way arrow to resize

Rotate text

Orientation

Format (eg add colour)

Alignment

Spacing

Return to gallery

Alternative shapes

Wrap document text round WordArt

Letter height

Figure 4.9

Drawings

You don't have to be a great artist to produce quite attractive effects using the Drawing toolbar options (see Figure 4.10). There are ready-made shapes (AutoShapes) – such as lines, rectangles, circles, arrows or stars – that are inserted in the same way that you insert Text Boxes; or you can use the freestyle 'pencil'. Once your shape is on screen, you can insert a border, fill it with colour, change its shape or position or flip or rotate it to point in a different direction.

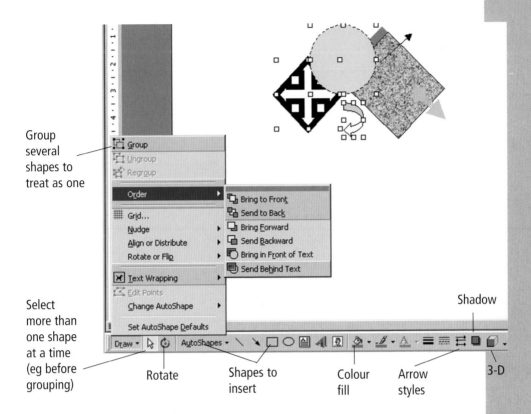

Group several shapes to treat as one

Select more than one shape at a time (eg before grouping)

Rotate

Shapes to insert

Colour fill

Arrow styles

Shadow

3-D

Figure 4.10

You can layer drawing objects on top of one another, and use the *Order* option to send one shape behind another or behind text already present on screen. (This is very important if you want to emphasise text within a coloured box and still read the words.)

As with pictures (see pages 33–37), selected objects show sizing handles and you must see these before any toolbar options take effect. Dragging a white sizing handle, for example, will change the shape; dragging a green circle (with the rotate option on) will change the direction.

As well as creating drawings yourself using the Word drawing tools, you can use a separate package such as Microsoft Paint available from the Start – Programs – Accessories menu. You can also insert images from Clip Art (see page 33), a CD-ROM, or the World Wide Web, or images that have been scanned in or produced using a digital camera if you have the equipment. Note that the colour or sharpness of different images will vary, depending on the software used to create them. Common image file types you may come across include TIFF (.tif), bitmap (.bmp), JPEG (.jpg) or GIF (.gif) (file extensions are explained on page 20).

Tables

Tables are an excellent way to display information and, if the borders are removed, can be used to create columns of text or numbers.

For example, the Secretary of the Hambledean Allotment Association produced a leaflet on plant infections, and displayed the details in table format (Figure 4.11).

Infection	Plants infected	Chemical name	Form
Galls	Azaleas	Bordeaux mixture	Powder
Peach leaf curl	Ornamental fruits	Lime-sulphur	Powder or suspension
Onion white rot	Onions	Calomel	Powder
Black spot	Roses	Cheshunt compound	Powder for solution
Rusts	Ornamental plants	Mancozeb	Wettable powder

Figure 4.11

To produce a similar table, click the Insert Table button 🔲 and drag the mouse across the number of squares ('cells') that you want in your table (Figure 4.12). Let go and the table will appear in your document. (Alternatively, you can go to *Table – Insert – Table* and enter the number of rows and columns you want.)

Type a heading in the first cell and then press the Tab key or use the mouse to click another cell. (Pressing Enter will move the cursor to the next line in the *same* cell.)

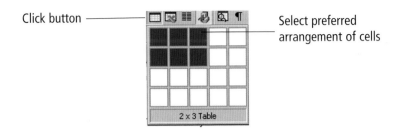

Click button —————— Select preferred arrangement of cells

2 x 3 Table

Figure 4.12

To delete a block of cells, click one cell and then go to Table – Delete – Column/Row. (If you select text in the table and press the Delete key, you will remove cell contents but leave the blank cells still visible.)

To insert further cells, click a cell, go to Table – Insert and pick the appropriate option, such as *Rows above* or *Columns to the left.* A quick way to add a further row at the bottom of the table is to click in the last cell and press the Tab key.

Click and drag the four-way arrow that appears in a little box at the top left of the selected table to drag it round the screen ✛ , and alter cell measurements by dragging a border when the pointer shows a two-way arrow.

Borders and shading for tables

After creating a basic table, you may like to add borders or shading effects. One way is to apply a ready-formatted design. *Right*-click the table and select *Table AutoFormat.* Scroll down the examples and select a design that you like. You can always change individual features later or deselect some of the format effects by removing the tick in the checkboxes (see Figure 4.13).

As an alternative, select parts or the entire table and apply colours or borders by going to *Format – Borders and Shading* (or *right*-click and select *Borders and Shading* from the short menu). You can even open a special toolbar – *Tables and Borders* – via the View – Toolbars menu. You can remove borders by selecting the *None* or *No border* setting.

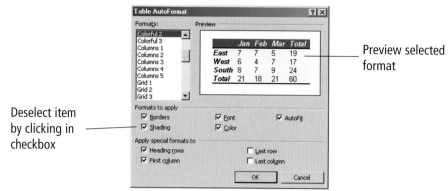

Preview selected format

Deselect item by clicking in checkbox

Figure 4.13

More advanced features

Once you start creating publications, you may find that you want to use more advanced features. This is the time to move on to a dedicated desktop publishing application – you will be offered galleries of design templates to customise, including business cards, complicated forms, calendars or even origami patterns. There are many packages to choose from, but three that are commonly available are Adobe PageMaker, Serif Page Plus and Microsoft Publisher.

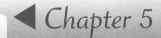

Chapter 5

Cards, posters and presentations with PowerPoint

When the visual effect of your work is just as important as the contents, a presentation package such as Microsoft PowerPoint becomes a valuable tool. With it you can produce professional-looking notelets, cards or posters, and you can accompany talks or lectures with overhead projector slides or even give a slide show on the computer itself. This chapter explains how to use PowerPoint for:

■ Posters
■ Making greeting cards
■ Giving a talk
■ Slide shows on the computer

The chapter concludes with a checklist of the key features of PowerPoint.

Starting out in PowerPoint

In PowerPoint your working area is known as a slide, rather than a page, and you can view it alone ('Slide view') or in 'Normal view' where it is alongside views of the textual content of the slide ('Outline') and any notes you may write to accompany a talk.

To produce a single item such as a poster, you might imagine that when you open the application you will be offered a blank screen and can start creating your artwork straightaway. Unfortunately there are a few things you need to do first:

(a) When you launch PowerPoint you have alternative starting points and need to select the most appropriate **presentation**. Choose Blank presentation, rather than the Wizard or Template, to give yourself a free hand. ('Wizards' are guides found in various

Microsoft applications that can help you produce files or objects step-by-step, but they are not necessarily always the best place to start.) You can always explore the other options once you are more familiar with the application.

(b) Choose the **layout** for your slide by scrolling through the Autolayouts displayed in the **New Slide** window that will have appeared automatically. Some layouts offer areas for inserting charts, pictures or columns of text in the form of 'placeholders' or you can select the completely blank slide.

(c) Decide on the **view** of the slide you want to work in. Select Slide view to work on the slide alone, or stay in Normal view and extend the boundaries of the slide area so that you can work with text, colours and images straightaway (see Figure 5.1).

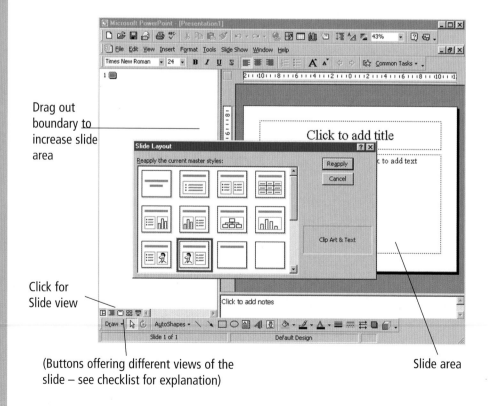

Drag out boundary to increase slide area

Click to add title

Click for Slide view

(Buttons offering different views of the slide – see checklist for explanation)

Slide area

Figure 5.1a Normal view

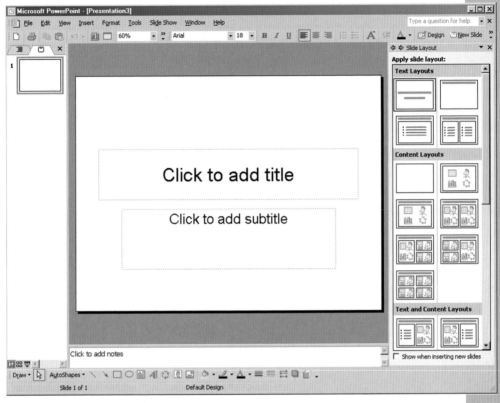

Figure 5.1b In PowerPoint 2002 slide layouts can be selected in a window at the side of the screen

The checklist at the end of the chapter on pages 80–82 explains the key features of PowerPoint and you can refer to it whenever you want to remind yourself how to carry out a particular task.

Posters

You saw in the previous chapter that you can produce attractive artwork using a word processing package. However, you will probably find that some of the display features in PowerPoint are even better for projects that are aiming for a real visual impact.

When producing any artwork, it is always a good idea to rough out the work on paper first. You will then know if you need to edit the text to balance the effect, where to place objects, and whether you need to find some pictures or photos in advance.

Orientation

If you need your poster in upright (portrait) A4 orientation, you will have to change your slide from the default landscape setting. Do this by going to File – Page Setup and clicking the correct orientation option.

Text

For an overall title, either create a WordArt object (see pages 58–60) or insert a Text Box (see page 35) and type the text as normal where the cursor is flashing. You will find that the box expands as you add more text, and that you can remove the surrounding border or emphasise it with choices from the *Line Color* and *Fill Color* buttons on the Drawing toolbar.

Extra toolbar buttons that you may like to use include those that increase or decrease the font size in single steps, making it easy to preview any changes, and another that adds shadow to selected text (see Figure 5.2).

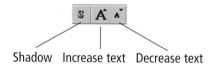

Shadow   Increase text   Decrease text

Figure 5.2

You can continue to add further Text Boxes until your poster displays all the relevant textual information

Images and colours

Insert some Clip Art by double-clicking the Clip Art button 📷 , or add an image from file using the shortcut button 🖼 or by going to the Insert – Picture – From File menu option and browsing through the files on your computer. After it appears, drag the selected image into position or resize it as necessary (see page 35).

One way to brighten up the whole poster is to go to Format – Background and choose a colour from the drop-down list (see Figure 5.3). You will find that an accompanying colour scheme has been applied automatically to lines, text and fill colours, but you can change any of these by going to Format – Slide Colour Scheme – Custom and selecting alternatives.

Colour scheme for selected background colour

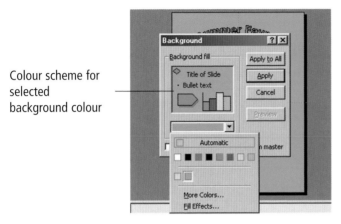

Figure 5.3

If you want borders, you can use the Rectangle or Oval Autoshapes on the toolbar to draw shapes around particular objects. You will probably find that the text or object disappears, but don't worry – either select Draw – Order – Send to Back/Send Behind Text to show your text or images against a coloured background, or click the Fill Color button and select *No Fill*.

Rectangle surround with no colour fill but a thickened line

Text in Text Box with no line colour

WordArt

Background colour added

Oval Autoshape filled with colour and sent to back

Clip Art

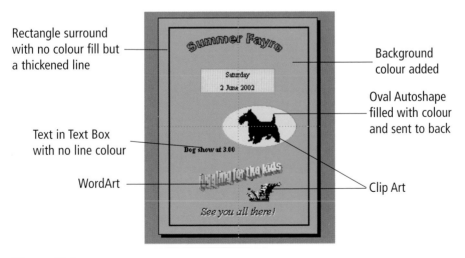

Figure 5.4

Making greetings cards

A simple card can be produced based on a single A4 sheet of paper folded down and then across, as in Figure 5.5.

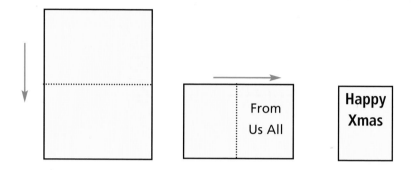

Figure 5.5

In practical terms, to print this properly you will need to create the card by dividing the page into four. The inside message will go in the top left-hand corner, where it needs to be flipped upside down, and the front picture and text will go in the bottom, right-hand corner (see example in Figure 5.6). If you want to, you can also add little pictures or extra text in the empty quarters.

Figure 5.6

Guides

To work in one quarter of the card at a time, make sure that the guide-lines are visible. If they are not present, go to the **View** menu and click the *Guides* option. These dotted lines won't appear when you print your card, but are very helpful when positioning your designs.

Flip and rotate

The front of your card is quite simple. Find a suitable image and insert and resize it together with WordArt or boxed text as you have done for the poster.

To produce inside text that won't be upside down in the finished card, first insert it in a Text Box and format it as normal. Click the box to select it and then click the **Free Rotate** button 🔁 on the Drawing toolbar. Four green circles will appear at the corners of the box. When you move your mouse over a circle, the pointer will change to a circular arrow and, as you click and drag, you can move the box round to a new position. Alternatively, select the Text Box and then click the **Draw** button on the Drawing toolbar and select *Rotate or Flip – Flip Vertical*.

If you want extra features on other parts of the card, add them and take care that they face the correct way up before you print your card and make the final folds.

To rotate a picture, it must first be converted into an object. You can do this by selecting the picture, going to *Draw – Ungroup* and then *Draw – Group*.

Giving a talk

Everyone gets nervous before giving a talk, but using PowerPoint means that at least your overhead projector slides will look professional. Also, the audience will be looking at your slides rather than you and it should therefore be less stressful than standing all alone on a stage.

Imagine that you have been asked to give a talk to a local community group about letting a property. You might come up with something like the following topics on which you want to speak, and which should therefore be made into slides:

Introduction	Furnishings
Finding the right property	Legal requirements
Purchasing	Pitfalls
Property management	Conclusion
Keeping track of money	

New slides

Once you have decided the order in which the topics will be covered, start designing the first slide and then add new slides with appropriate layouts.

With your first slide in front of you on screen, click the **New Slide** button ⏚ . Slide Number 2 will appear and you can go backwards and forwards between the slides by clicking the Previous or Next Slide arrows on the right-hand side of the screen (see Figure 5.7), or pressing the Page Up and Page Down keys.

Slide contents (outline view)

Previous/Next Slide

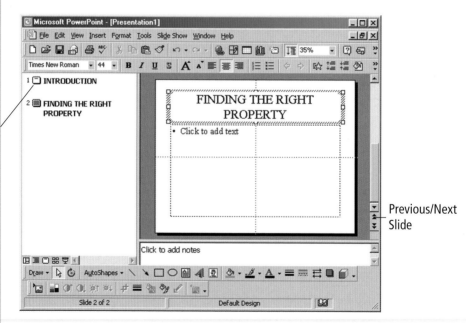

Figure 5.7

Using the Masters

To give your slides a 'consistent' feel, you may want to include a logo or WordArt object on every slide. Rather than adding the item to each

72

slide individually, PowerPoint provides an overall template in the form of a Slide Master. If you make changes or add anything to this slide, the change will be visible on every slide throughout the presentation.

To add a picture of a house to every slide, for example, view the Slide Master by clicking **View – Master – Slide Master** (see Figure 5.8). Insert Clip Art or a drawing of a house. You can then make any other changes you want, such as to the font or bullet styles for example. These will be duplicated on all your slides and you can now return to Normal or Slide view by clicking the appropriate view button.

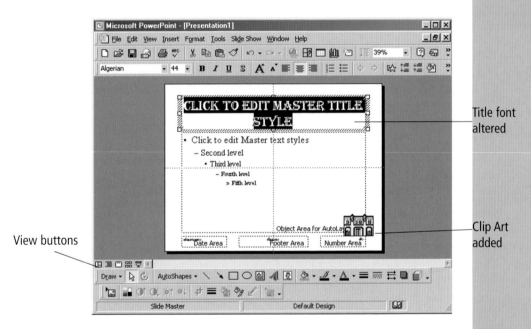

Figure 5.8

Organisation charts

As PowerPoint was created for business uses, there is an organisation chart option designed to display company structures that can be very useful in other contexts, such as showing any kind of hierarchy or family tree.

To use it for an appropriate slide – such as for a different talk on kings and queens, genealogy, plant families etc – either apply a slide layout with an organisation chart placeholder that you can double-click, or

73

select **Insert – Picture – Organisation Chart.** You will automatically open the application *Microsoft Organisation Chart 2.0* showing a basic 'tree' that you can customise in a variety of ways:

- Click any box to add your own text, and amend the chart title.
- Select a different level (eg one labelled 'co-worker' or 'subordinate') and then click the correct box to attach another alongside or below it in your tree.
- Choose an alternative arrangement of boxes from the **Style** menu.
- Alter box borders or colours from the **Boxes** menu and alter links between boxes from the **Lines** menu.
- Add a background from the **Chart** menu.

When the chart is finished, select **File – Close and Return to** (*name of presentation*), making sure you save it by selecting the option to update the chart before closing. Return to the program at any time by double-clicking the chart.

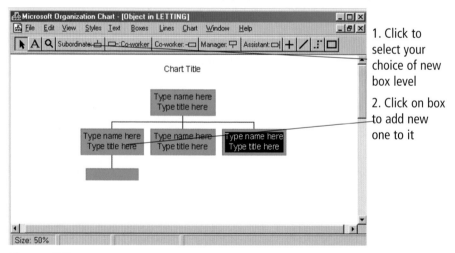

Figure 5.9

Numerical charts

You can add graphs or numerical charts (see pages 100–104 for more details) in just the same way. This time, select a suitable slide layout and double-click the placeholder, or go to **Insert – Chart**, and a basic spread-sheet and chart will appear floating over the slide (see Figure 5.10).

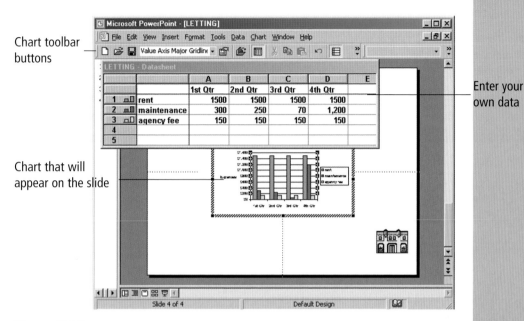

Chart toolbar buttons

Enter your own data

Chart that will appear on the slide

Figure 5.10

Change the data in any of the cells, select an alternative chart type if you prefer, or add colours or borders, and then click *outside* the chart to return to your slide. To make changes, double-click the chart to display the appropriate toolbars and spreadsheet data again.

Notes for the speaker

To help you as you give your talk, you can create reminders in the form of small thumbnail pictures of your slides accompanied by word-processed notes. Select the View – Notes page, or click in the lower section of the Normal view screen, and enter your reminders in the box provided.

Printing options

If you click the *Print* toolbar button, you will print one copy of each of the slides in your presentation. To choose any other option, you need to open the Print dialog box by selecting *File – Print*. In the *Print What:* box you can now choose to print individual slides, notes pages or the outline of your talk. You can also print two, three or six thumbnail pictures of your slides grouped together on single sheets of paper, to hand out to your audience before or after your talk, by selecting the *Handouts* option.

Colour effects

As different printers react rather differently to the acetate sheets used for overhead projectors, you should check carefully that you are using the appropriate type of sheet before you print. This may mean that you can't use a colour printer. You can check what the presentation looks like in black and white by clicking the greyscale preview button .

If you do want to use the full colour effects, perhaps to print out a version of your presentation in the form of a coloured booklet, or to add a light background colour to your slides, you can not only change individual backgrounds and borders, but you can also apply complete design templates (see overleaf).

Slide shows on the computer

If you have recently attended a conference or exhibition, you may well have seen a slide display appearing on a computer or screen in the corner. It is very easy to create such a slide show with PowerPoint, but you would need to check that you had an appropriate projector and screen, or large-screen monitor, for it to be visible to all your audience.

There are several advantages to running your slide show on the computer itself:

■ The audience will be concentrating on the visual effects and just listening to your voice in the background, so it is excellent for the shy talk-giver.
■ You can make full use of the animation, colour and sound facilities in the package.
■ As long as you sort out the timings and slide progression, it is more relaxing than changing slides as there is no risk of dropping them or getting them out of order.

Views of your presentation

To design and then show your Lettings presentation on the computer, you need to know about two further views:

Slide Sorter view displays all the slides at once. It is very useful for rearranging your slide order (just click any slide and drag it to a new position) and for viewing the effect on all your slides of changes to the overall colour or design.

Slide Show removes the toolbars and menus and is the way to preview and then run through the complete presentation. Press the Escape key to leave the show.

Applying designs

There are a range of templates, in the form of combined background colours and designs, that you can apply to all your slides by going to Format – Apply Design Template and selecting the design you like in preview (see Figure 5.11).

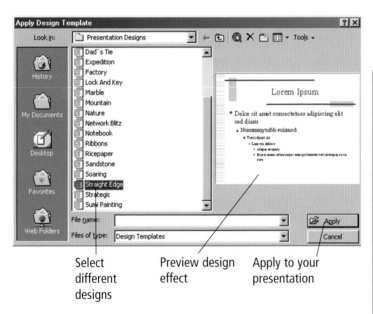

Select different designs

Preview design effect

Apply to your presentation

Figure 5.11a

Figure 5.11b In PowerPoint 2002 you can apply templates by going to Format – Slide Design. You will see a window like this at the side of your screen

77

If there are particular aspects you then want to change, you can do this on the Master Slide or via the **Format – Background** or **Slide Colour Scheme** menu options. You can also change the design at any time by reopening the *Apply Design Template* window and choosing a different template.

Transitions

To start with, each slide will simply replace the previous one during a Slide Show when you click the mouse or press Page Down or Enter. To make the show more interesting, you can choose exactly how each slide will appear (see Figure 5.12).

For example, you may like the idea of a slide appearing slowly from the top or bottom of the screen, or revealed as if Venetian blinds have been opened. Selecting **Slide Show – Slide Transition** can set these 'transitions' from one slide to another and the same or different transitions can be applied to each slide in the show. You can even accompany the transitions with sound effects and set the slides to appear automatically after a certain number of seconds, so that you don't need to operate the mouse or keyboard.

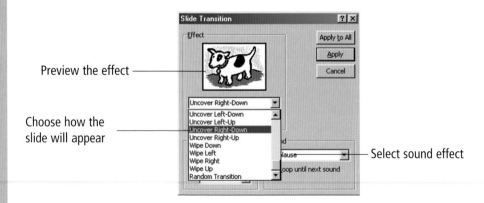

Figure 5.12

Animations

Even more interesting effects can be achieved if the various items on any one slide are built up during the show itself – for example, words flying in from the corners or images exploding into place, once again accompanied by sound effects. To achieve this, you need to select **Slide Show – Custom Animation**.

For your chosen slide, click the *Effects* tab to select the appropriate type of entry or sound effects etc for any item (eg cash register sounds to accompany the finances chart), as shown in Figure 5.13. Then click *Order & Timing* to choose in which order each item will appear and whether it requires a mouse click or will appear automatically. The funniest effects can be achieved by positioning an item (eg a cartoon drawing) in the grey area *next* to the slide, as it can be made to fly or crawl across the screen and disappear from view.

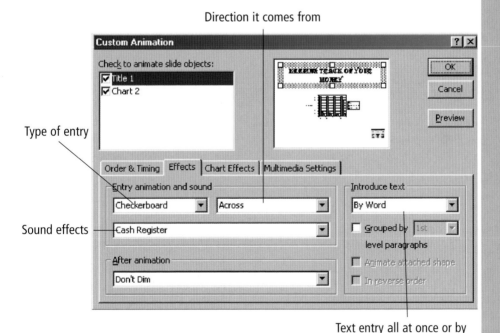

Figure 5.13

Checklist

Checklist of key features of PowerPoint

Launching PowerPoint	Double click the icon ▣ or go to Start – Programs – Microsoft PowerPoint.
Creating the first presentation	■ Select *AutoContent Wizard* to base your presentation on a ready-written template. You can customise some of the opening screens but will need to replace most of the text to meet your own needs. ■ Select *Design Template* to select a background or presentation from those listed. ■ Select *Blank Presentation* for single items (eg cards, posters, invitations, etc) or to build up a presentation slide by slide.
Create the first slide	Select a layout from the New Slide dialog box and click OK.
Amending slide layout	To apply a different layout, click *Slide Layout* ▤, select an alternative and click OK.
Add a second/subsequent slide	Click the *New Slide* button ▦, select a layout and click OK.
To move between slides	Click the up or down arrows to the right of the slide ▤ to go backwards or forwards through your presentation. You can also press the Page Up or Page Down keys.
Start a new presentation	Click the *New* ▯ toolbar button.

Save a presentation	Click the *Save* button 💾 and select the location and name for the file. All slides, notes, charts, etc will be saved together in a single file.
Open a presentation saved earlier	Click the *Open* 📂 toolbar button and browse through your files to find the one you want.
Views of your presentation	🔲 *Normal* – the outline, slide and notes are all visible on screen together. ☰ *Outline* – to work on the text alone. 🗖 *Slide* – to concentrate on text, colours and images. 🔠 *Slide Sorter* – to see thumbnail pictures of all your slides together. 🖵 *Slide Show* – to remove toolbars and watch slides with any accompanying sound and animation effects. *View – Notes Page* – add notes for the speaker under a small slide picture. *View – Master – Slide Master* – add entries once, and they will appear on every slide in the presentation.
Add text to a slide	■ If you choose a layout with a text placeholder, just double-click and enter text as directed. ■ Click the *Text Box* button 🖹 and draw a box in any space on the slide. Add text where the cursor is flashing – the box will expand as you type.

To emphasise text	▪ Click the text to pick up the Text Box border, then add lines or shade the background using the Drawing tools (see pages 60–62).
	▪ Select text and use normal toolbar or *Format – Font* menu options. There is an extra *shadow* button ⑤ also available.
	▪ Select the text and then click the appropriate button to increase or decrease font size in steps. Up A A Down
To alter paragraphs	▪ Click arrow buttons to promote ⬅ or demote ➡ text to different levels of heading (for example within a bulleted list).
	▪ Close up or widen spacing between lines of text using toolbar buttons ⬆⬇.
Insert pictures or WordArt	See relevant sections on pages 33–37 and 58–60.
Print your presentation	Select *File – Print* and choose whether to print: some or all of the slides; just the outline; handouts with thumbnail pictures of the slides; or notes pages.

Chapter 6

Spreadsheets, charts and databases

Even if you don't regard yourself as particularly numerate, it is surprising how often you will be performing quite complex calculations. Have you planned a journey using bus or train timetables, for example? Do you check the total before paying your shopping bill or the waitress in a café? Did you work out how much fertiliser you needed to buy for your size of garden, or how many tins of paint were required to decorate the kitchen?

Spreadsheet applications such as Microsoft Excel are very straightforward and extremely useful for some of the everyday calculations you may want to make. This chapter introduces the main features of Excel, and concludes with a checklist of the key features. It looks in particular at:

- Creating a spreadsheet
- Finding the best value
- Keeping track of your expenses
- Projections
- Creating a chart
- Creating a database

Creating a spreadsheet

Spreadsheets comprise column or row headings or labels, together with the numerical data – either raw figures or the results of calculations performed within the application. You can use a spreadsheet as a short-term calculator, or save the file (known as a 'workbook', consisting of a number of 'worksheets') and keep it for months or years both for reference and to update the figures.

When you open Excel, instead of a plain white screen as in Word, you will see what looks like a sheet of squared paper. Letters and numbers mark the columns and rows of squares, and each square – known as a 'cell' – has the address of its column letter and row number (eg B2 or C3).

	A	B	C
1	£26		
2	£34	B2	
3	£29		C3
4	£32		
5			

Figure 6.1

At any time, one cell will have a black border. When you type text or numbers, they will automatically appear in this cell, which is therefore known as the *active* cell. You can move round the sheet very easily using the mouse or keyboard to 'activate' different cells, and thus enter data in different columns or rows.

Once the basic data has been entered, you can change its appearance in a similar way to formatting text in word processing. Click any cell, or select a range of cells with the mouse when the pointer shows a white cross, and then use the toolbar buttons (eg **B** or <u>U</u>) to embolden or underline entries, or add £ symbols or extra decimal places to numerical data. More detailed options are available from the Format – Cells dialog box.

To make sure that every entry is visible, you may need to widen columns or alter the height of a row. Move the mouse pointer over the boundary between the header letters or numbers and drag the boundary in or out when the pointer changes to a two-way arrow.

In Excel, you do need to remember to *finish* entering data in a cell – either press the Enter, tab or cursor key or click the mouse in another cell – before trying to make any changes. Otherwise the menu options will appear faded and you won't be able to make your selection.

Calculations

Once you have entered some data, such as the details of your weekly milk bill (see Figure 6.2), you can use Excel to carry out various calculations. To do this, you need to type instructions (a 'formula') into any cell in which you want the answer to appear.

To check your weekly bill, calculating the cost of milk each day involves multiplying the number of pints by their price and displaying the answers in cells D3 – D9. To find the total for Monday, you would enter the following formula in cell D3:

$$=B3*C3$$

The = symbol is required as it instructs the software to carry out a calculation. You then type the 'address' of the cell containing the number of pints followed by the correct 'operator' (* means multiply – see page 109 for accepted operators) and then the address of the cell containing the cost of each pint.

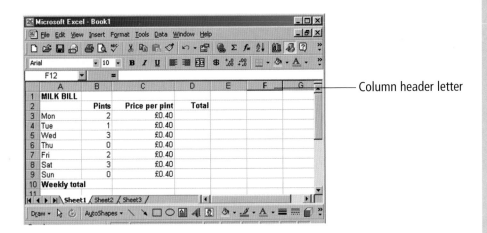

Column header letter

Figure 6.2

Entering cell addresses rather than the figures themselves means that, if you alter the data, the calculations will be updated automatically.

When you press Enter, the answer 0.80 will appear in the cell. This formula can then be copied down column D to work out the cost of milk for the other days in the week.

Copying formulae – or any cell contents – is quick using the mouse. Click on the cell containing the first example of the formula or entry to be copied and then move the mouse over the small black square showing in the bottom, right-hand corner of the cell. The pointer will now be visible as a black cross +. Click and hold down the mouse button and drag the cross down the column or across the row.

Totals

To produce an overall total for the week, you need to add up all the answers in column D and produce a final result in cell D10 (see Figure 6.3). In this case, if you entered each cell address separately, it would take too long as the formula would need to be written:

$$=D3+D4+D5+D6+D7+D8+D9$$

Instead, use the quick method to total a number of cells using a special set of instructions built into Excel known as a *function*. (All the functions are available if you click the Paste Function button f_x.)

The SUM function to add up entries for all cells in the range D3 to D9 is entered as:

$$=SUM(D3:D9)$$

(You can type SUM in upper or lower case but there should be *no* spaces, and brackets and colon must be entered correctly.)

You can even click the AutoSum button (Σ) to enter this function into the cell automatically (see checklist on page 110).

To check that a formula has been entered correctly, activate the cell and look in the long window above it, which is called the Formula Bar. This shows any formula entered into a cell (rather than the result of a calculation) as well as normal text or number entries (see Figure 6.3). To correct a mistake, click in the Formula Bar or double-click the cell and delete/retype entries.

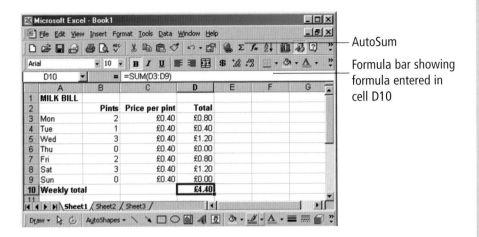

AutoSum

Formula bar showing formula entered in cell D10

Figure 6.3

Saving spreadsheets

There may be a number of sheets in any one workbook that you can open and use by clicking the *Sheet* tab at the bottom of the screen, and these will be saved automatically when you save the file. However, it is best to open a new workbook every time you want to create a spreadsheet on a different topic so that its filename will be listed when you search your files in the future.

Save workbooks exactly as you save Word documents – click the **Save** toolbar button and choose an appropriate location and name for your file.

Printing spreadsheets

Although spreadsheets comprise hundreds of columns and rows of cells, you will only print the small area in which you have been working. Nevertheless, having created a number of columns, your spreadsheets may be too wide to print onto a single piece of paper. To prevent a small spreadsheet printing onto more than one page, check first in Print Preview and, if necessary, alter the page orientation to *Landscape* or click *Fit to 1 page* in the File – Page Setup – Page dialog box.

Finding the best value

Although many large supermarkets now display shelf labels showing the exact cost of 100 grams (g) of every type of pasta, cheese or cat food, your local corner shop may not be so helpful. So you may like an easy way to discover if a 400g tin of *Chompey* at 45p is cheaper than a 375g tin of *Yummy* at 40p, or if three for the price of two of expensive *Dollop* is better value than three packets of *Cheapo* at the normal price.

You can use the same method for many other calculations – for example, whether holiday A is better value than holiday B, taking into account the various supplements and discounts, or whether material 54" wide is going to leave less waste than material 36" wide when covering your sofa.

Let's use the example of buying cereal. This can come in a range of packages, from large boxes to individual portions. Although there is an optimum size to buy because it becomes stale quite quickly, it would be nice to know that your favourite size and brand is also the best value. You may be surprised to find that biggest isn't always best.

Here are the three basic steps:

- List each brand and size of cereal box, together with its price, and enter these into three columns on your spreadsheet.
- Type in the correct formula to work out the price of the same units (eg 100g) for every cereal.
- Sort the data to display the cereal manufacturers and packet sizes in order, from cheapest to most expensive.

Creating the spreadsheet

Here are some typical cornflake packet sizes and prices. The weights have all been converted into grams (ie 1 kilo = 1,000g) and then entered into a spreadsheet, shown in Figure 6.4:

Formulae

Price for 100g: The formula to calculate this in Column D is the price of *one* gram of cereal (ie the price of each packet divided by the number of grams it contains), multiplied by 100.

For the 1,000g pack of Brand X cereal, this is written =**C2/B2*100** and you can copy this formula down the column to work out the cost for all the other packets (see page 86 for how to do this). After formatting the numbers to show two decimal places (see checklist on page 109), the spreadsheet data looks like this (Figure 6.4):

	A	B	C	D
		Size (g)	Price (£)	Price per 100g
1	Name			
2	Brand X	1000	1.77	0.18
3	Brand X	250	0.75	0.3
4	Brand X	500	0.94	0.19
5	Brand X	750	1.38	0.18
6	Brand X variety pack (8)	136	1.29	0.95
7	Own brand	1000	1.19	0.12
8	Own brand	500	0.79	0.16
9	Own brand	750	0.99	0.13
10	Own brand healthy eating	250	0.69	0.28
11	Own brand value	500	0.47	0.09
12	Own brand variety pack (8)	136	0.98	0.72
13	Brand Y organic	375	1.09	0.29

Figure 6.4

Sorting (re-ordering) data

So that prices are not split from their brands, you must first select *all* the data. Then open the Sort dialog box by selecting Data – Sort.

Sort by *Price per 100g – Ascending*, and, if you included the headings when you selected the data, leave the default *My List has Header Row* selected so that this row is not included in any re-ordering (see Figure 6.5). Then click OK. The results are shown in Figure 6.6.

Figure 6.5

The results

	A	B	C	D
	Name	**Size (g)**	*Price (£)*	**Price per 100g**
1	Own brand value	500	0.47	0.09
2	Own brand	1,000	1.19	0.12
3	Own brand	750	0.99	0.13
4	Own brand	500	0.79	0.16
5	Brand X	1,000	1.77	0.18
6	Brand X	750	1.38	0.18
7	Brand X	500	0.94	0.19
8	Own brand healthy eating	250	0.69	0.28
9	Brand Y organic	375	1.09	0.29
10	Brand X	250	0.75	0.3
11	Own brand variety pack (8)	136	0.98	0.72
12	Brand X variety pack (8)	136	1.29	0.95

Figure 6.6

The results reveal the very high cost of buying small variety packs and the large disparity in price between a 250g pack of cereal and the 500+ g sizes. However, it is comforting to know that, if you don't *want* to buy a kilo of cereal at a time, you may only be paying an extra 1p per 100g if you stick to 500g boxes of your favourite brand.

Keeping track of your expenses

A spreadsheet can be very useful for displaying everyday income and expenditure clearly and simply; it allows you to see exactly where your money is going. It may seem a tedious task to put all your finances onto a spreadsheet, but once you have created the basic layout, you will find that entering expenditure or details of income becomes almost routine, and so useful that you'll wonder why you didn't do it before.

You might want to keep all your finances in one workbook file, using a new sheet each year, or create a new file each time. You could also produce one master copy and then customise it each year, or simply make a copy of last year's spreadsheet, delete the cell entries and then save the headings as a new version for this year.

Formatting a spreadsheet

To give you an idea of the process, Figure 6.7 shows a very simple imaginary budget based on the following items:

Expenditure
- Rent
- Heating
- Telephone
- Clothes
- Petrol
- Council Tax
- Food

Income
- Pensions
- Part-time job
- Interest on savings
- Money made from car boot sales

	A	B	C	D	E	F	G	H	I	J	K	L	M	N
1		Single Person's Budget												
2		Expenditure								Income				
3		Rent	Heating	Telephone	Clothes	Petrol	Council Tax	Food	Total	Pensions	Part-time j	Interest	Car boot s	Total
4	April													
5	May													
6	June													
7	July													
8	August													
9	September													
10	October													
11	November													
12	December													
13	January													
14	February													
15	March													

Figure 6.7

Wrap text

To stop the spreadsheet stretching endlessly across the screen, you may want to restrict the width of the columns. However, some of the headings may be quite wide and still need to be fully displayed. The answer is to 'wrap' the text down the column:

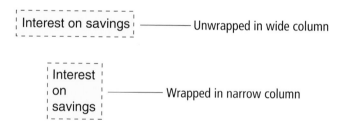

Enter the full text into one cell (where it may appear to spread across other columns), select the cell and then go to Format – Cells – Alignment. Click the *Wrap text* check box under *Text control* and the entry should now appear wrapped down several lines.

You may still need to amend the column width (eg to prevent words being split) but can keep it far narrower than would otherwise be the case.

Vertical alignment

The header row will now be far deeper, and other headings may only take up one line. To display these attractively, select the cell and, from the Format – Cells – Alignment dialog box, align the text vertically at the top, bottom or centre of the cell.

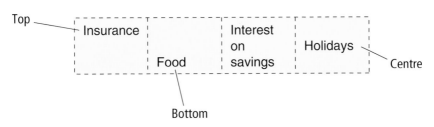

Figure 6.8

Centred headings

If you want main or sub-headings to be centrally placed above the relevant data, you can use the **Merge and Center** toolbar button 🈴 .

Enter the heading in one cell, and then select the cells across the width of the data (see Figure 6.9).

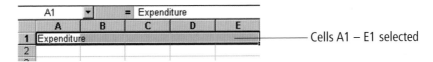

Figure 6.9

Click the **Merge** button and the heading will 'jump' into the centre of the selected cell area. It will look as if the heading is in cell C1, but it is in an enlarged A1 and the next cell is now F1 (see Figure 6.10).

Figure 6.10

Freeze panes

Once a large spreadsheet has extended beyond the width or bottom of the screen, it can be very annoying to use, as you have to scroll back and forth to check that you are entering your data into the correct row or column.

The answer is to 'freeze' the headings. Then, as you scroll down or across, headings remain on screen and the data temporarily disappears underneath them.

To keep the months in view, click B1 (ie the cell to the *right* of where you want the frozen pane to appear) and then go to **Window – Freeze Panes** (see Figure 6.11). Now as you scroll across to column E and F, earlier columns will disappear underneath column A (Figure 6.12).

	A	B	C	D	E	F
B1		=	Single Person's Budget			
1		Single Person's Budget				
2					Expenditure	
3		Rent	Heating	Telephone	Clothes	Petrol
4 April		400	50	20	35	25
5 May		400	45	20	10	18
6 June		400	38	20	40	16
7 July		400	39	20	0	30
8 August		400	25	20	65	10
9 September		400	60	20	15	35
10 October		400	68	20	0	40
11 November		400	80	20	0	35
12 December		400	75	20	65	28
13 January		420	80	20	0	30
14 February		420	60	20	23	26
15 March		420	45	20	44	34

Figure 6.11

	A	D	E	F
I15		=		
1		et		
2			Expenditure	
3		Telephone	Clothes	Petrol
4 April		20	35	25
5 May		20	10	18
6 June		20	40	16
7 July		20	0	30
8 August		20	65	10
9 September		20	15	35
10 October		20	0	40

Scroll across to view further columns

B – C hidden under A

Figure 6.12

To freeze the category headings instead of the months, you would need to click cell A4. To freeze both headings *and* months, you would click B4 (ie the cell to the right and below where the fixed lines should be drawn.)

To remove the freeze, select Window – Unfreeze Panes.

Auto format, borders and shading

For a spreadsheet that you will constantly refer to, it is important that columns and rows are displayed clearly and attractively. A simple method is to realign headings, reformat text to stand out (eg increase the font size and make it bold) and border and shade selected blocks of cells (see Figure 6.13). Either use the toolbar buttons, or go to Format – Cells – Border or Patterns.

Borders   Fill colours

	Rent	Heating	Telephone	Clothes	Petrol	Council Tax	Food	Total	Pensions	Part-time job (net)	Interest on savings	Car boot sales
				Expenditure						**Income**		
April	400	50	20	35	25	55	100	685	450	160	61	300
May	400	45	20	10	18	55	180	728	450	160	63	180
June	400	38	20	40	16	55	90	659	450	160	59	
July	400	39	20	0	30	55	210	754	450	160	61	525
August	400	25	20	65	10	55	150	725	450	160	59	
September	400	60	20	15	35	55	265	850	450	160	56	
October	400	68	20	0	40	55	210	793	450	160	59	250
November	400	80	20	0	35	55	200	790	450	160	62	465
December	400	75	20	65	28	55	175	818	450	160	66	
January	420	80	20	0	30	55	220	825	450	160	69	
February	420	60	20	23	26	55	205	809	450	160	64	
March	420	45	20	44	34	55	185	803	450	160	72	348
Overall total	4860	665	240	297	327	660	2190	9239	5400	1920	751	2068

Figure 6.13

An alternative is to choose from one of the ready-made template designs available from the *Format – AutoFormat* menu. Pick a layout and take off any formatting options you don't want applied before clicking OK.

Using the spreadsheet

If you enter all standing orders and regular payments when the spreadsheet is first created, plus the formulae to calculate totals and the difference between income and expenditure, you can keep an eye on the changing totals every time you enter new data. You will therefore be in a better position to say whether you can afford a particular item, or to plan where to cut back if it looks as if you will run out of money before Christmas or some other expensive time. You can also insert extra columns very easily if you find you need further categories, but make sure that your formulae take these new cells into account.

Projections

Another useful facility with spreadsheets is to be able to ask 'what if'. You can see from the example above that it is very easy in Excel to change some of your figures and see what effect this has on your expenditure or income. There are many other situations where the ease of creating different scenarios is very helpful.

One example might be the decision whether or not to hold more meetings of your social club during the year. Your income from the refreshments would rise, but the cost of the hall may well mean that you make a loss at the end of the day. Should you put up membership fees to cover any gap?

In this example, the aim is to make at least £300 per year to pay for the annual outing and Christmas party.

Present position

Membership fees	£10 per annum
Number of members	65
Hall hire each meeting	£35
Meetings per year	6
Cost of purchasing tea per meeting	70p
Income per person from refreshments	20p
Members attending (on average)	25

The spreadsheet shown in Figure 6.14 provides the following information (with profit/loss calculated by taking the contents of cell H7 away from H4).

	A	B	C	D	E	F	G	H
1	Social Club Details							
2	Income							
3	Membership fee	No. members	Income from membership	Refreshments	No. buying tea	No. meetings	Tea income	Total income
4	10	65	650	0.2	25	6	30	680
5	Expenditure							
6	Hall hire	No. meetings	Hall costs		Tea	Expenditure on tea		Total Expenditure
7	35	6	210		0.7	4.2		214.2
8							Profit/Loss	465.8

Figure 6.14

If you double the number of meetings held each year, the final profit falls below £300 (see Figure 6.15).

	A	B	C	D	E	F	G	H
1	Social Club Details							
2	Income							
3	Membership fee	No. members	Income from membership	Refreshments	No. buying tea	No. meetings	Tea income	Total income
4	10	65	650	0.2	25	12	60	710
5	Expenditure							
6	Hall hire	No. meetings	Hall costs		Tea	Expenditure on tea		Total Expenditure
7	35	12	420		0.7	8.4		428.4
8							Profit/Loss	281.6

Figure 6.15

The following projections are both ways to maintain a balance over £300 and can be used to help decide on the best course of action:

Scenario 1 – increase membership by £2 and possibly lose five members (see Figure 6.16).

	A	B	C	D	E	F	G	H
1	Social Club Details							
2	Income							
3	Membership fee	No. members	Income from membership	Refreshments	No. buying tea	No. meetings	Tea income	Total income
4	12	60	720	0.2	25	12	60	780
5	Expenditure							
6	Hall hire	No. meetings	Hall costs		Tea	Expenditure on tea		Total Expenditure
7	35	12	420		0.7	8.4		428.4
8							Profit/Loss	351.6

Figure 6.16

Scenario 2 – leave membership fees as they are and hold only nine meetings a year (see Figure 6.17).

	A	B	C	D	E	F	G	H
1	Social Club Details							
2	Income							
3	Membership fee	No. members	Income from membership	Refreshments	No. buying tea	No. meetings	Tea income	Total income
4	10	65	650	0.2	25	9	45	695
5	Expenditure							
6	Hall hire	No. meetings	Hall costs	Tea	Expenditure on tea			Total Expenditure
7	35	9	315	0.7	6.3			321.3
8							Profit/Loss	373.7

Figure 6.17

Absolute cell addresses

It is necessary to produce accurate results quickly when exploring what would happen. In the above example, the best way to see the effect of running 6, 9, 12 or 15 meetings per year would be to include one cell in your spreadsheet that held the number of meetings. This cell would be referred to in all your formulae and any change of the number would be reflected automatically in your totals. For this to work, you have to fix the *absolute* cell address in your formulae.

For example, if you were selling plants at a local fête and wanted to see the effect of increasing your prices by a certain percentage, you could create the following spreadsheet to display last year's figures (see Figure 6.18).

D6		= =B6+C6		
	A	B	C	D	E
1					
2	% increase	0%			
3					
4					
5	Plants - box of 10	Cost	Extra %	Final cost	
6	Tomato	£3.00		£3.00	
7	Pepper	£5.00		£5.00	
8	Basil	£4.50		£4.50	
9	Thyme	£6.00		£6.00	
10	Broad bean	£3.50		£3.50	
11	Runner bean	£4.00		£4.00	
12					

Figure 6.18

To find out the effect of a 5% increase on all the prices, you can change the entry in B2 to 5%. The formula in C6 to work out the extra 5% becomes =B6*B2 (see Figure 6.19).

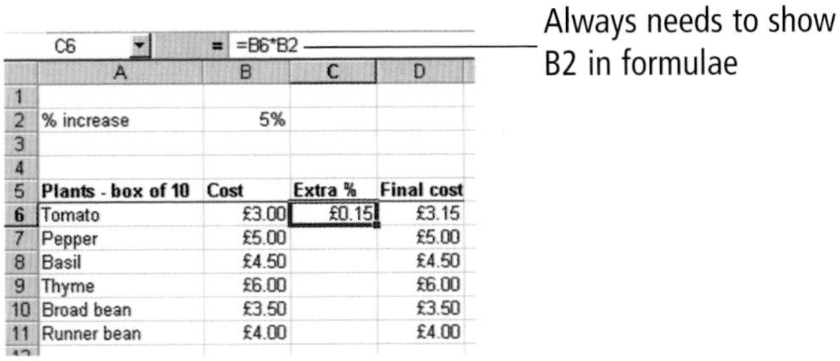

Always needs to show B2 in formulae

	C6	▼	=	=B6*B2		
	A		B	C	D	
1						
2	% increase		5%			
3						
4						
5	Plants - box of 10		Cost	Extra %	Final cost	
6	Tomato		£3.00	£0.15	£3.15	
7	Pepper		£5.00		£5.00	
8	Basil		£4.50		£4.50	
9	Thyme		£6.00		£6.00	
10	Broad bean		£3.50		£3.50	
11	Runner bean		£4.00		£4.00	

Figure 6.19

However, if you copied this down column C in the normal way, it wouldn't work. This is because the extra % for Pepper in C7 would show =**B7*B3**, C8 would show =**B8*B4** and C9 would show =**B9*B5**. In other words, copying down would apply to B2 as well as B6 and the results would be completely wrong (see Figure 6.20).

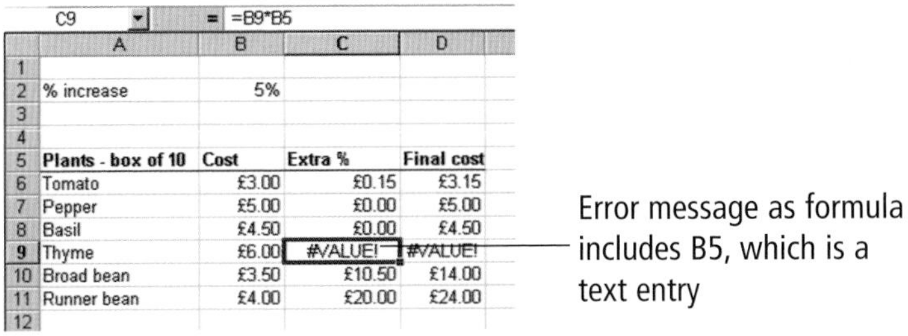

	C9	▼	=	=B9*B5		
	A		B	C	D	
1						
2	% increase		5%			
3						
4						
5	Plants - box of 10		Cost	Extra %	Final cost	
6	Tomato		£3.00	£0.15	£3.15	
7	Pepper		£5.00	£0.00	£5.00	
8	Basil		£4.50	£0.00	£4.50	
9	Thyme		£6.00	#VALUE!	#VALUE!	
10	Broad bean		£3.50	£10.50	£14.00	
11	Runner bean		£4.00	£20.00	£24.00	
12						

Error message as formula includes B5, which is a text entry

Figure 6.20

Instead, you have to 'fix' the position of B2 in the first formula *before* copying down. All the formulae will then be accurate. This is done by manually or automatically inserting dollar ($) signs in front of the column letter and row number of the cell involved. (Take care – leaving out one $ will mean the column or row that follows is not fixed.)

There are two ways to fix absolute cell addresses:

1 Enter the correct formula =B6*B2 in C6, but manually insert $ signs in front of the B and 2 so that it appears =**B6*B2**.
2 Alternatively, enter the normal formula and, in the Formula Bar, click the mouse between the B and the 2 and press function key F4. This enters the dollar signs automatically (see Figure 6.21).

99

Figure 6.21

You can now copy the formula down the column and all the formulae will include a reference to cell B2. Also, whenever you change the amount in B2, the calculations will be updated automatically (see Figure 6.22).

Figure 6.22

Creating a chart

It can often be easier to 'read' charts and graphs than figures, and so it is very helpful for sharing information if you can produce a pictorial view of your data. Certainly if you ever give talks, help in a local school, work for a charity or act as any kind of adviser, you can get your message across far more easily if you display charts rather than numbers.

If you help at your local school, for example, you could be asked to carry out a survey of the pets the children have in their households. The information is entered into an Excel spreadsheet and needs to be displayed in chart form (Figure 6.23).

	A	B	C	D	E	F	G	H
1	Cats	Dogs	Birds	Rabbits	Gerbils	Fish	Snakes	**Stick insects**
2	10	7	3	5	8	16	1	6
3								

Figure 6.23

To produce a chart, select the cells, including any headings, and click the Chart toolbar button ▥. You will now be taken through four steps to create your chart. Either click *Next* to move on or *Back* to amend any actions:

1 Select the chart type (eg Column) and click the preview button to check its overall look.

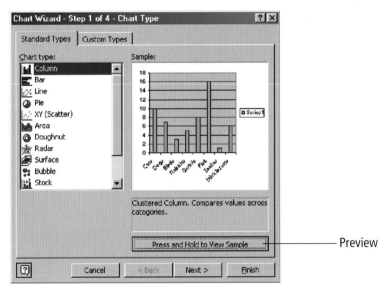

Figure 6.24

2 Check that the correct data has been included (if not – reselect data) and that the headings you want along the bottom (X axis) are displayed.

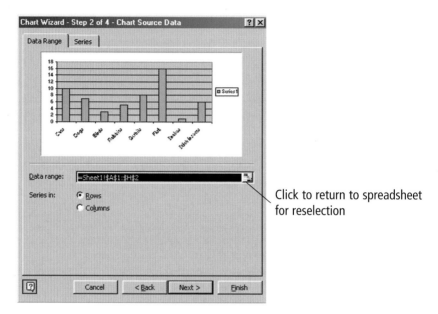

Click to return to spreadsheet for reselection

Figure 6.25

3 Add titles for main chart and axes, and if you don't want the 'legend' (key), click the **Legend** tab and de-select *Show Legend*.

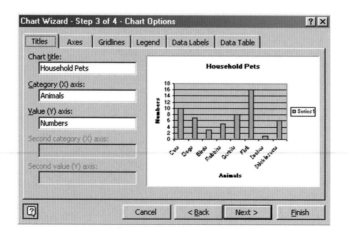

Figure 6.26

4 You can choose to display the chart on the same sheet as the data or separately on its own sheet.

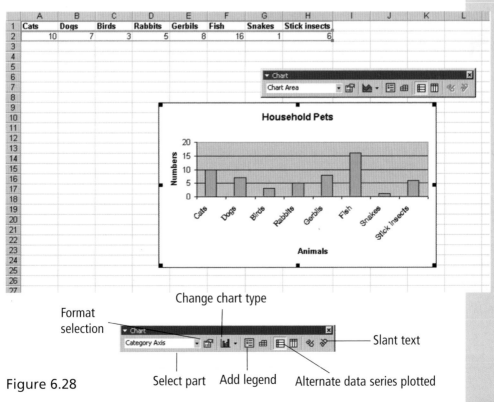

Figure 6.27

The finished chart will appear on screen, together with a Chart toolbar for amending its appearance (see Figure 6.28). Some options (eg to add any titles you omitted by mistake) are also available from the Chart – Options menu.

Figure 6.28

You often need to resize a chart to show all the labels clearly – just click and drag any border over a sizing handle. You can also select any part (such as the chart area, titles or axis labels) to reformat, colour or realign. Either *right*-click to produce a short menu, double-click or click the appropriate toolbar button or menu option.

One of the most difficult things to decide is which is the best chart type for your needs. Running through the different types can help you decide. Figure 6.29 shows an example of a pie chart.

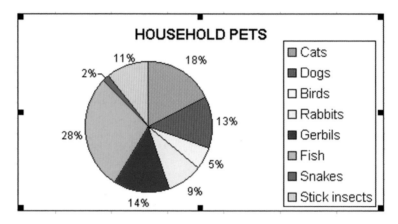

Figure 6.29

Printing a chart

Select the chart with one mouse click if you want it without the related data. Otherwise, both spreadsheet and chart will be printed together if you placed the chart on the same sheet.

Copying charts into other documents

It is very easy to copy across a chart when producing documents in Word, for example. Open the Excel worksheet holding the chart, select it, click *Copy* and then return to Word and *Paste* it into your work. It will remain available in the Clipboard until you close your program.

Creating a database

To keep track of people's addresses, your record collection or the range of plants in your garden, you can use Excel to create a simple database. It will be easy to maintain and can be searched in a matter of seconds.

Unlike Microsoft Access, which is one of the most widely used database applications, Excel cannot be used to create tables of data that can be linked and searched in detail. However, you can make use of its facilities to produce databases that are perfectly adequate for simple, everyday record-keeping.

Many people work as volunteers in the community, and if you have such a job in a charity shop, for example, it is quite likely that you could be asked to help set up a database of clothes or books that are on sale. Then, when a customer phones up and asks for a particular item, you can search the database to check whether you have it in stock and, if so, how much it will cost.

Setting up the database

The data is set out just as in any normal spreadsheet, with category headings (fields) in the top row and each row representing a single record. It could look something like the following example (Figure 6.30).

	A	B	C	D	E
1	Children's Clothes				
2	Item	Average age	Colour	Price	Number in stock
3	Skirt	6	Blue	£3.00	1
4	Shirt	10	Check	£2.50	4
5	Shorts	7	Black	£1.75	10
6	Skirt	8	Pink	£4.00	1
7	Jumper	5	Yellow	£6.50	20
8	Blouse	9	White	£3.50	5
9	T-shirt	4	Blue/green	£2.00	5
10	T-shirt	9	Red/yellow	£2.50	8

Figure 6.30

Searching

Using a form allows you to display a single record at a time, or you can use a filter to show all matching records. In both cases, you can either search for items that match entries exactly (eg all *Skirts* or anything

Yellow), or you can base your search on entries you type in yourself using criteria that include logical statements (eg *Less than £5* or *Not blue*).

Forms

To create a form as a way to display your records, select the headings and all the data in the database and then go to **Data – Form**. A form will appear showing details of the first record, and you can move through the records using the *Find Next* button.

To find all the Yellow clothes, click the **Criteria** button. The data will disappear and you can type in *Yellow* in the empty Colour box. Now click *Find Next* and the next relevant record should be displayed (see Figure 6.31).

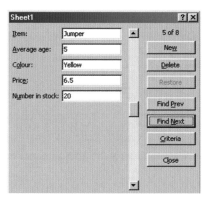

Figure 6.31

Using * symbol to represent any missing characters, and maths symbols for more than > or less than <, you could search for any items that have Blue at the beginning of the colour and a price that is less than £4 (for example). (*Don't* type the £ symbol in the box, just simple numbers.)

Using filters

To display more than one record at a time, select the database entries and then go to **Data – Filter – AutoFilter**. You will see small boxes appear next to each heading that, when clicked, display all the entries in that particular field (see Figure 6.32).

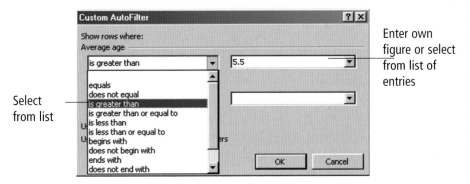

Children's Clothes

Item	Average a	Colo	Pri	Number in sto
Skirt		(All)	£3.00	1
Shirt	10	(Top 10...)	£2.50	4
Shorts		(Custom...)	£1.75	10
Skirt	8	Black	£4.00	1
Jumper		Blue	£6.50	20
Blouse		Blue/green	£3.50	5
T-shirt		Check	£2.00	5
T-shirt		Pink	£2.50	8
		Red/yellow		
		White		
		Yellow		

Figure 6.32

To search for all records matching one entry, click an example in the appropriate field.

To enter your own criteria, click the (*Custom...*) entry for a chosen field. You can now select a logical statement and choose a definite match or enter your own choice in the main window (see Figure 6.33).

Select from list

Enter own figure or select from list of entries

Figure 6.33

To display all the records again, go to *Data – Filter – Show All* or click (All) in the field list.

Checklist

Checklist of the basic spreadsheet operations in Excel

Launch Excel	Double-click the icon ⊠ , or select *Start – Programs – Microsoft Excel.*
Start a new workbook	Click the New 🗋 toolbar button.
Save a workbook	Click the Save 🖫 toolbar button and select the location and name for the file.
Open a workbook saved earlier	Click the Open 🗁 toolbar button, browse through your folders, select the file and press Enter.
Move round spreadsheet	■ Click any cell for data entry.
	■ Press Enter to move down column.
	■ Press Tab to move right along row.
	■ Hold Shift and press Tab key to move left along the row.
	■ Press arrow keys to move in specific direction.
	■ Scroll up/down or left/right using the scroll bar arrows.
	■ Press Home to move to the first cell in the row.
	■ Hold Ctrl as you press Home to move to cell A1.
Select cells	■ Click any cell – it will show a black border and is called the 'active cell'.
	■ Click and drag across rows or down columns to select several adjacent cells. The pointer shows a white cross and the active cell remains white.

	■ Click the grey box between heading letters and row numbers to select the complete spreadsheet.
Format text in cells	■ Click cell and then use toolbar shortcuts (eg **Bold**, *Italic*). ■ Go to *Format – Cells – Font*.
Format numbers in cells	■ Click cell and use toolbar shortcuts (eg % or +. 0). ■ Go to *Format – Cells – Number* and select *Currency* or *Number*, and set the appropriate number of decimal places.
Change alignment in cell (the default is text on left and numbers on right)	■ Click cell and use toolbar alignment buttons. ■ Go to *Format – Cells – Alignment*.
Formulae – accepted operators	■ Add + ■ Subtract – ■ Multiply * ■ Divide / ■ ALL formulae start with = ■ Either enter the cell address manually, or click any cell when typing a formula and its address will be added automatically.
Checking calculations are correct	■ Always carry out a rough estimate. ■ Click the cell and check the formula in the Formula Bar.

Ways to total cell contents (eg in A5)	■ **=A1+A2+A3+A4** ■ **=SUM(A1:A4)** ■ Select range and click AutoSum button Σ to insert the result in the next empty cell. ■ Click in the cell in which you want the result to appear and then click Σ

	A	B	C
1	£26		
2	£34	**B2**	
3	£29		**C3**
4	£32		
5			

Averages	**=AVERAGE(A1:A4)**
Copy cell contents (eg for formulae making use of the *relative* position of cells)	■ Select cell. ■ Move pointer to the black square (fill handle) in the bottom, right-hand corner of the cell. It will show a black cross + ■ Hold down mouse and drag + down column/along row. ■ Let go and check entries have copied correctly.
Enter incremental steps (eg *Jan, Feb, March* or *8, 9, 10* or *7, 14, 21* etc)	■ For simple numerical increments, hold Ctrl as you copy down with the + ■ To copy *dates*, enter the first in one cell and then copy down as normal with the +. Excel will recognise a date series. (To *prevent* this happening for repeating the same date, enter it twice, into *two adjacent cells*, and then highlight both cells and copy down from the second.)

	■ To increase numbers by unusual increments, enter two consecutive numbers in adjacent cells and then highlight both and copy down from the second.
Move cell entry to a different cell	■ Move mouse over active cell border until it shows a white arrow. Click and drag to new position. ■ Use normal *Cut & Paste* and then press Escape key to remove flashing dots round original cell.
Copy entry to a different cell	■ Enter =(*address of original entry*) eg =**A3** ■ Hold down Ctrl as you drag with the white arrow. A small + sign will be visible. ■ Use normal *Copy & Paste* and press Escape key to remove flashing dots round original cell.
Alter column width	■ Move mouse between heading letters *above* the column until it shows a two-way arrow. Click and drag right-hand boundary left or right. ■ Click any cell and select *Format – Column* menu option.
Alter row height	■ Position pointer between row heading numbers on the left of the screen and drag edge up or down with the two-way arrow. ■ Select any cell and choose *Format – Row* menu option.
Insert columns or rows	■ Click column letter heading or row number heading to select the

	complete column/row, and then go to *Insert – Column/Row*. The new column/row will 'slide' into place and heading letters/numbers will adjust automatically.
	■ Select a particular number of rows or columns, such as four to insert four new rows or columns.
Delete columns or rows	■ Click the column heading letter or row number to select the complete column/row and then go to *Edit – Delete*. (Pressing the Delete key will only delete cell *contents*, and not the entire column/row.)
Print spreadsheet	■ Check first in *Print Preview*.
	■ Click *Setup* button to change page orientation or click *Fit to one page* option.
	■ Click *Print*.
	■ To print a portion of a spreadsheet, select the area and, in the Print box, select *Print selection*.

Chapter 7

The Internet and the World Wide Web

We are all used to the fact that we can talk to people in other countries on the phone, as long as they have access to the international telephone system. The Internet is simply networks of computers that can communicate with one another. At the present time, most computers are connected to the Internet via the telephone cable system, but in the future it may be more common to connect via mobile phones, televisions or satellites.

There are two main uses for the Internet – sending and receiving electronic messages (emails), which will be covered in Chapter 9, and viewing documents displaying text, pictures, video clips or sound. These multimedia documents make up the World Wide Web (referred to as the Web or WWW) and so the pages are known as Web pages.

This chapter looks at:

- Connecting to the Internet
- Searching the Internet
- Bookmarks
- Saving and printing Web pages

Connecting to the Internet

In order to send or receive information via the Internet, you need three things:

1 **An Internet Service Provider (ISP).** You register with this company and it then provides the programs and dial-up facilities to enable you to send and receive emails and view Web documents. It may also offer space on its computer for your own small Web page. Examples of ISPs include Tesco, Woolworths, AOL, Virgin, BT and Demon.

2 **A browser.** This is the software installed on your computer that displays Web documents. The two common browsers are Netscape and Internet Explorer and one of these may already be installed, or will be provided free by your ISP. (The examples in this book relate to Microsoft's Internet Explorer.)

3 **A modem.** The hardware inside, or attached to, your computer that enables computerised data to be sent down telephone lines. Most computers on sale today will already have a modem installed.

ISPs offer two different kinds of service: some ask you to pay a monthly fee and then provide several hours of free connection to the Internet each month. Others give you free registration and software, but you have to pay a local telephone charge every time you connect and go 'online'. Choosing the best option depends on how many hours a month you think you are likely to spend browsing the Web for information, but you can always change your ISP if your first choice isn't right for you.

ISPs are everywhere – building societies, bookshops, supermarkets and other large retailers offer the CD-ROMs in their stores that you need to get connected, or you will find disks on the front covers of computer magazines or even sent out via direct mail. Registering is quite easy if you insert the CD-ROM into your D: drive and follow the on-screen instructions. You will be asked for an identifying name – your username or ID – and a password that for security purposes will be displayed as a row of ******. (On your own computer, you will be able to set the machine to remember these automatically so that you won't need to enter them every time you connect to the Internet.)

One decision to make before you register is how you would like your name displayed in your email address. Sometimes your 'username' will have to be two names separated by a dot eg *John.Mitchell*, or you might be able to choose *jmitchell*, *John_Mitchell* or even simply *John*. If you have a common name, you may be told that someone else already has your chosen combination of names in their address, and you may be offered the rather annoying option of mixed names and numbers (eg *John.Mitch24*). For this reason, it is worth noting down a few more acceptable (and memorable) alternatives that you can fall back on before you start the registration process. (See Chapter 9 for more details about using the email system.)

Once you have registered, you can connect to the Internet by double-clicking the browser icon added to your Desktop 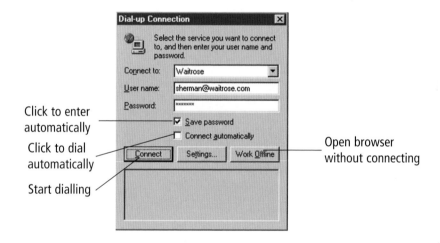. A small window labelled *Dial-up Connection* (see Figure 7.1) will open. It will show your name and password and you must select **Connect** to get online. This option, too, can be set to start automatically if you wish, and you can also open the browser window but stay unconnected by clicking the button labelled **Work Offline**.

Click to enter automatically

Click to dial automatically

Start dialling

Open browser without connecting

Figure 7.1

Saving money

For most home computer owners who do not take out a regular subscription with an Internet Service Provider, the cost of using the Internet is the same as using the phone for a local call. You must get into the habit of disconnecting from the Internet every time you finish a session. Close the browser window and click *Disconnect* in the dialog box that will appear.

There are other things you can do that will also help save money:

1 Ask your phone company to give you itemised bills so you can keep an eye on how much you are spending on Internet calls.
2 Try to connect at the cheaper rate times (ie evenings and weekends).

3 Add the ISP phone number you are dialling to any special savings schemes (eg BT's 'Family and Friends').

4 If you dial a special number to make savings and give a small percentage to a favourite charity, make sure that you dial this prefix when connecting. Set this up by going to Start – Programs – Accessories – Communications – Dial up Networking. Double-click the icon with the name of your ISP on it, then click the Dial Properties button. In the small boxes labelled *To access an outside line: for local/international calls dial:*, enter your extra numbers and click Apply (see Figure 7.2).

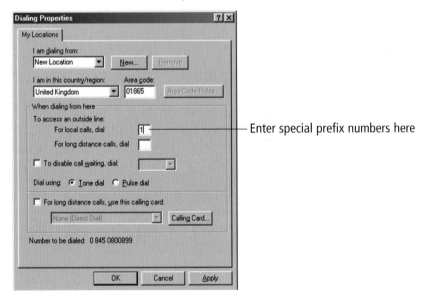

— Enter special prefix numbers here

Figure 7.2

5 If you come across an interesting article that you want to read, double-click the flashing computer icon visible on your taskbar and click the Disconnect button. When you have finished reading and want to carry on searching, click a hyperlink (see page 118) and you should get a Connect dialog box up again (see Figure 7.3).

Figure 7.3

6 When writing emails (see Chapter 9 for further information), stay offline and choose to send each message later. The messages will be collected together in your outgoing mailbox and, when you have finished all your emails, they will be sent in one go when you click the Send/Receive button.

7 Try not to phone your ISP's help desk too often, as technical support is often very expensive.

Web pages

When the browser window opens you will see familiar menus together with some special toolbar buttons, and in the main part of the screen there will be a Web page (Figure 7.4). Different Web pages open (in a process known as 'downloading' where they are temporarily saved onto your computer) as you locate information on the Web, but every time you launch your browser the same opening page will appear. This is known as your 'home page' and is usually a page on the Web site of your ISP.

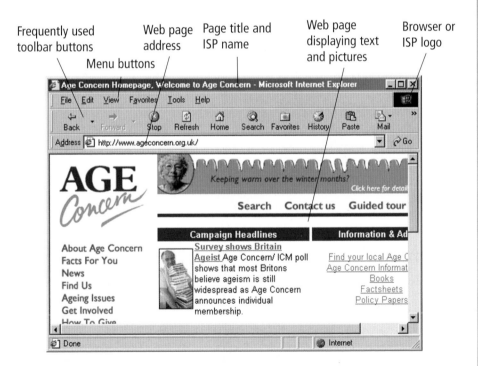

Figure 7.4

Most Frequently Used Toolbar Buttons

Back	Press this to return to the previous page
Forward	Reopen a page you came back from
Home	Return to your opening home page
Stop	Halt the downloading of a page
Refresh	Reload the page
History	A list of sites you have visited in the past
Favorites	Shortcuts to selected sites you choose to keep note of
Address	The address or location of the Web page displayed on screen

Hyperlinks

There are two basic methods for opening new Web pages: manually changing the address in the Address window; or clicking a 'hyperlink'.

As you move your mouse pointer over a Web page, you will see that at various points it changes from an arrow to a hand 🖑 . When this happens, you will open a new page if you click the left mouse button. Clickable text or images are known as hyperlinks and are placed in Web pages through the use of special code (called HTML) which is written into the page when it is created. The new page will be directly relevant to the hyperlink you clicked and will also contain links to other, related pages.

Web page addresses – URLs

Every Web page has an address (its URL or Uniform Resource Locator) where it is stored and where people surfing or browsing the Web can access it ('access' is the term used for finding and opening a Web page on your computer screen). To open any page, all you need to do is enter the URL of the page into the Address box at the top of the browser window and press Enter. The browser logo in the corner of the window will revolve as the page is located, and it will then be downloaded and displayed on your screen.

Fortunately, there is a standard way of addressing pages that can help you to 'guess' the URL and open a page of interest to you. For example, the URL for Age Concern England is:

http://www.ageconcern.org.uk

There are four main parts to the URL:

http://	Means the page follows the code or protocol by which Web pages are transferred onto the Internet. (In most browsers, you don't need to type this when entering a URL in the Address box.)
www	Refers to pages on the World Wide Web
ageconcern	Is the registered name of the organisation (there is no need to use upper case letters in URLs as they are case insensitive)
org.uk	Shows that it is a UK organisation such as a charity

Although there are plenty of exceptions, the URLs of most British companies end co.uk whereas national or local government departments end gov.uk. Most international companies end .com, which is why so much is written about 'dot com companies', and educational establishments can be either ac.uk (British) or .edu (American). New extensions are added all the time, however, and you may now find URLs ending .biz for businesses or .name for private individuals, for example.

The name plus ending or extension in any URL is known as the 'domain name' and well-known domain names include:

bbc.co.uk
ukonline.gov.uk (government information service)
microsoft.com
vso.org.uk (Voluntary Service Overseas)
london.ac.uk (London University)
tesco.co.uk

So if you wanted to find out opening times at Hamleys store, you might guess correctly that the Web address would be *www* then the name of the store *hamleys* and then *co.uk* for a British company, ie
www.hamleys.co.uk

If you type the most likely URL into the Address box and you get it wrong, you will see a message saying the page could not be found. Try again, altering the registered name slightly and perhaps changing *org.uk* to *co.uk*, or *co.uk* to *.com*. You must also make sure that you have entered the punctuation, such as the *dot* between words, accurately.

Sometimes you won't be able to open the correct page because the registered name of the organisation is not straightforward (eg the URL for the Automobile Association is **www.theaa.org.uk** not **www.aa.org.uk**). In such cases, you will have to find the URL by another route, as described below.

Searching the Internet

There are millions of Web pages on the Internet that might contain useful information. Unless you know the organisation that published the pages and its URL, you will need help in locating relevant Web sites.

There are three main ways you can locate information – gateways, directories or search engines.

Gateways

These sites contain links to information on a specific theme (eg *education*, *health* or *the environment*). If you open up the gateway page, you can either scroll through the categories and listed sites until you come across those of relevance to your query, or you can enter your search criteria in the box provided.

For example, you may want to find out everything you can on osteoporosis. If you enter the URL **http://healthweb.org** into the Address box and press Enter, and then click on the *Women's Health* category, you will be able to access sites covering osteoporosis that you can visit by clicking them with the mouse (see Figure 7.5). Web sites change constantly but one search of *healthweb* yielded two such sites.

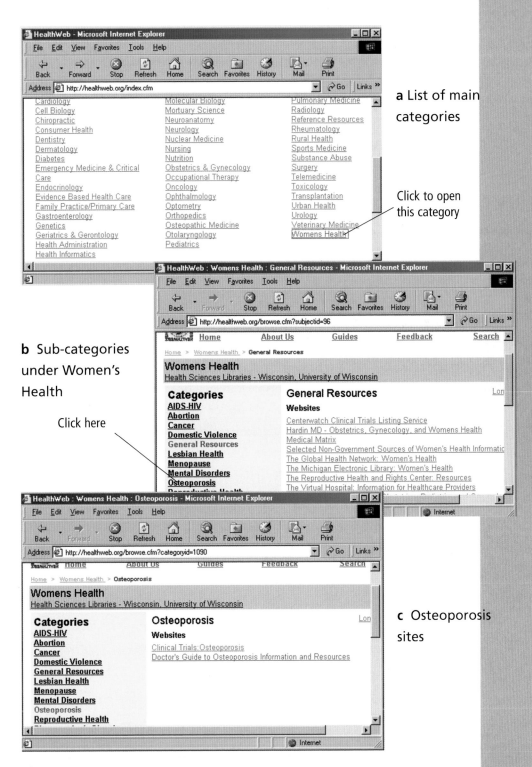

a List of main categories

Click to open this category

b Sub-categories under Women's Health

Click here

c Osteoporosis sites

Figure 7.5

Other gateways you might like to visit include:

- another medical and health gateway known as OMNI at **http://omni.ac.uk**
- the AstroWeb Astronomy Gateway at **www.stsci.edu/science/net-resources.html**
- ADAM covering art, design, architecture and media information at **www.adam.ac.uk**
- a History gateway at **www.ihrinfo.ac.uk**
- Vetgate, useful for any information on animals at **http://vetgate.ac.uk**

Directories

These sites work by classifying Web sites under more general categories. Once again, you can work your way down through the headings and subheadings until you reach a restricted number of sites on your topic that have been selected for inclusion by the directory team. As there is no standard method for classifying Web sites (unlike the Dewey library system, for example), it may be difficult to locate information on a topic if it could come under various headings – for example would local IT training courses be classified under *regional*, *computers* or *education*? However, for discrete information, directories can provide useful lists of sites that are of manageable length.

To take the example of osteoporosis: you would need to click the *health – diseases* hyperlink and work through the alphabetical sub-categories (or type *osteoporosis* in the box provided). One search, using the **www.yahoo.com** directory, found 62 sites to visit (see Figure 7.6).

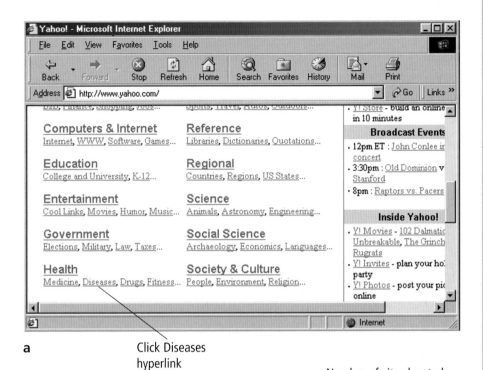

a   Click Diseases
hyperlink

Number of sites located

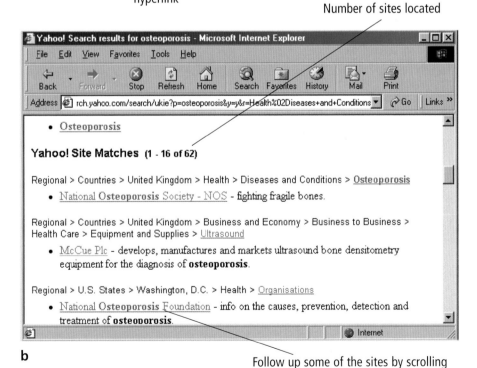

b

Follow up some of the sites by scrolling
down the list and clicking a hyperlink

Figure 7.6

Search engines

The most common method for locating information on the Web is to type words or phrases – known as 'keywords' – into the 'query box' provided by a search engine. There is no limit to the relevant sites they find as they are simply looking for an exact match within a huge database of Web pages.

In the case of osteoporosis, for example, entering the word into the query box provided by **www.altavista.com** resulted in a list of 140,485 sites (see Figure 7.7). Don't worry if your searches result in a similar number of matches (often referred to as 'hits'). The most relevant sites will appear on the first few pages of the list, and they are usually arranged 10 or so to a page. You should also be able to read a few words taken from the Web page and the date when it was last updated which will help you decide whether or not to click the hyperlink and download a particular page onto your screen. If you access a site and find the information unhelpful, just click the Back button in your browser window to return to the list.

Keyword searches

There is quite an art to typing in keywords – the more careful you are, the better the list of sites will be. It is often a case of trial and error but the following general advice may help:

- Put phrases between "speech marks" to stop words being searched for independently (eg "*dog trainers*" rather than *dog* and *trainers*, as this could otherwise locate sites about dog breeds and running shoes).
- Add UK (if there isn't a country checkbox you can click) if you want to limit your search (eg for goods and services) to this side of the Atlantic.
- Add + in front of words that must be contained, or – if they should not. For example *Coxes apples – recipes* should allow you to find out about the history or growth of this fruit but stop cookery pages being listed.
- Use AND to search for pages where words must be present, or AND NOT to filter out sites that contain particular words.

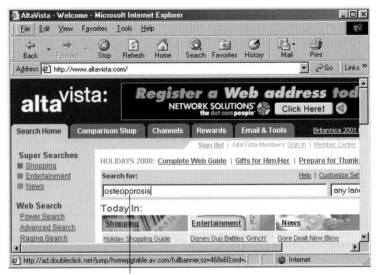

a

Type your keyword or phrase into
the query box and press Enter

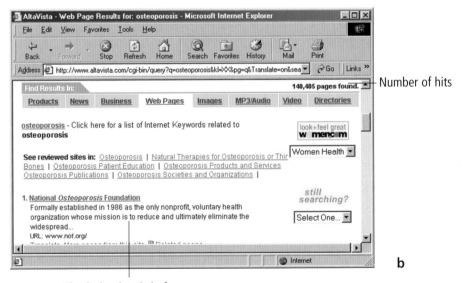

Number of hits

b

Check the details before
you follow up any site

Figure 7.7

- If you want a general search, you can use the * symbol to represent a range of letters. For example *join** should result in sites mentioning *joinery, joints* or *joining*.
- If you aren't sure about the best keywords to use, try typing an actual question, as the search engines usually ignore small words such as *the, in, and* or *where,* etc.

Useful sites for carrying out a search

Everyone has their favourite Web sites that they visit regularly when searching for information. A few examples are listed below. Some of these sites act as both directories and search engines and others, such as Megaspider, search the search engines. You will soon find that you compile your own list:

www.altavista.com
www.google.com
www.excite.com
www.yahoo.com
www.mamma.com
www.megaspider.com
www.lycos.co.uk

Bookmarks

As you search for information and follow up various hyperlinks, you will constantly stumble upon excellent Web pages that you know you will want to revisit. Rather than trying to remember the full URL, browsers offer a useful filing facility where you 'bookmark' your page and can return there with one click of the mouse.

Adding bookmarks

Bookmarked pages are filed in the Favorites folder in Internet Explorer (called Bookmarks in Netscape). A quick way to add the URL of the opened Web page is to hold Ctrl and press D. Alternatively, you can click the Favorites toolbar button, click *Add to Favorites* and check that the page title has appeared in the Name box (see Figure 7.8). If you find the title too long and unwieldy, click in the box and change the wording. Now select a suitable folder in which to file your book-marked page, or even create a new folder especially to hold it, and click **OK**.

When you want to open the page another day, click the **Favorites** tool-bar button, open the named folder and then click the bookmarked page name.

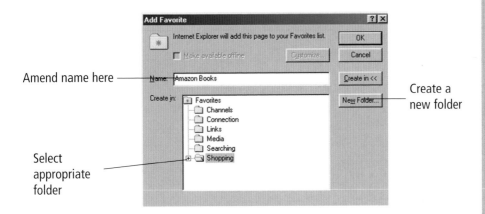

Amend name here

Create a new folder

Select appropriate folder

Figure 7.8

Organising your bookmarks

To keep your bookmarked pages tidy, you may want to reorganise or rename the pages and folders in your **Favorites** menu. (This is espe-cially true if you have added a page to the **Favorites** folder using Ctrl plus D, as it will just have been tagged on the end of the list of folders.)

To do this, click the **Favorites** button and then select **Organize Favorites** (see Figure 7.9). Locate any Web page or folder you want to delete or rename and click the appropriate button. To move a book-marked page to a different folder, select it in the window and click **Move to Folder**. You can then find the correct folder to click in the *Browse for Folder* window that will appear.

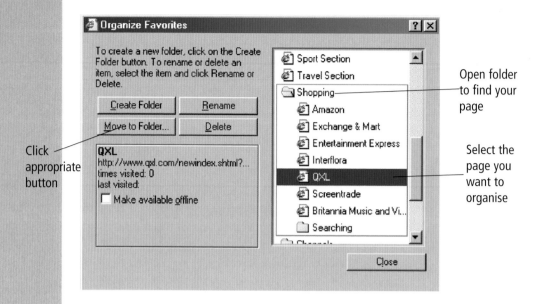

Open folder to find your page

Click appropriate button

Select the page you want to organise

Figure 7.9

Saving and printing Web pages
Saving

It is very easy to save a complete Web page onto your own computer, to read again, send as an email attachment or print out on paper. Just press the **Save** toolbar button 💾 and you will be offered the usual **Save As** box. You will see that the page will be saved as a Web page file – ending .html – and it will open up in the browser window when you go to read it another day.

Many of the 'words' on a Web page are actually image files and if you want to save these, or more straightforward pictures, drawings or photos, you need to *right*-click the image and select the **Save Picture As** option. In the **Save As** box, you will see that the file type is displayed as .jpeg or .gif (the two common Web image file types) and you should leave these as set. You will be able to open up any of these image files in Microsoft *Paint* (which will probably already be installed on your computer) or a similar graphics application, and you can then print them, copy and paste them into your documents or presentations or even use them on your own Web page (as long as no copyright is infringed).

Printing

Printing a Web page is also straightforward as you just click the Print toolbar button 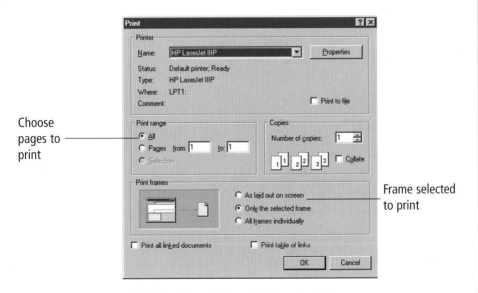 or go to File – Print and select the pages and copies you want.

However, you should be aware of two things when printing a Web page:

1 The length of one Web 'page' is difficult to gauge, and is not the same as one standard Word document page (ie an A4 piece of paper). You may therefore find yourself printing out very many pages of material you don't actually want. To prevent this happening, you can set the *Page range* to print *Pages 1–1* and then print pages 2, 3 etc if you want the extra detail that has not yet printed.
2 Many Web pages are divided into sections ('frames') and you need to check which frame(s) will print, to make sure that the information you want is actually going to print out. Usually, if you first click the section of interest, it will be selected to print alone unless you change the settings in the Print box (see Figure 7.10).

Choose pages to print

Frame selected to print

Figure 7.10

Downloading

On some occasions, you may be asked if you want to *download* pro-grams. This is the technical term for transferring files from the Internet onto your own computer and is perfectly safe if they come from an established Web site. Often you need the programs before you can make the most of sound or moving images on a Web page. They can also replace older versions of software (eg your browser) or may be necessary for playing games. For example, you may need to download a file transfer program such as CuteFTP (available from the Web site **www.cuteftp.com**) if you ever want to publish your own Web pages.

Downloading can take a few minutes or much longer. You will be asked where you want to store the files and then you need to stay online as they are transferred.

Chapter 8

What you can do on the Web

The exciting thing about the World Wide Web is that it is expanding and diversifying all the time. If Web sites on particular areas of interest weren't available a few months ago, they may well have appeared and be accessible today. Unfortunately, this dynamism is also a disadvantage, as established Web sites can disappear as rapidly as new ones are created. So please bear in mind the fact that sites mentioned in this book may not actually exist by the time you try to visit them.

In this chapter you will find details of a range of Web sites that may be of interest to people over 50. However, in the long term the most important task is for you to use search engines, follow up hyperlinks or visit sites that you have heard about or seen mentioned in newspapers or magazines, so that you can build up your own personal list of favourite and useful Web pages.

The chapter looks specifically at using the Web for:

- Shopping
- Finance
- Learning online
- Sharing an interest
- Keeping informed
- Playing music
- Games
- Sites for older surfers

Shopping

You can buy almost anything on the Internet nowadays and online purchases are becoming as commonplace as buying through a mail order catalogue or over the telephone. As long as you take the usual precautions, it should be as safe as high street shopping and usually much less time-consuming. You won't be able to examine the goods closely, of course, but you should always be able to return them if they turn out to be unsuitable.

Finding what you want

Once you have decided what to buy, you need to visit the right site, locate the exact items and then follow the online procedure for placing your order and confirming delivery or postage details. Usually you will select items by adding them to a 'basket' or 'trolley' and will move to the 'checkout' when you are ready to pay by credit card.

For own-brand items, or if you prefer to buy from well-known companies such as W.H. Smith, Sainsburys, Argos etc, there will be only one Web site to visit. However, many items are offered by a number of retailers and buying the cheapest or best quality may require some detective work. You can either use a search engine to locate the range of retailers offering the product, or use a specialist search facility.

For example, if you wanted to buy a book on Urdu poetry, you could visit a number of high street bookshops that have set up Web sites, such as Blackwells or Waterstones, or you could access one of the more well-known booksellers on the Internet, such as Amazon or Books online (**www.bol.co.uk**). Alternatively, there is a free service offered by Book Brain (**www.bookbrain.co.uk**) which carries out a search for you and finds the best bargain:

- Firstly you access the site and enter your keywords in the query box.
- From the books listed, you click the one you want to buy.
- This results in a shortlist of booksellers offering the book at the cheapest prices, taking into account delivery charges (which can be very high for a single item).
- Click on the bookshop name to go to its Web site.
- Click the **Add to Basket** button to put the book title in a 'virtual' shopping basket.
- You can continue to search the site and add other items until you are ready to buy all your chosen items.

- Clicking **OK** usually takes you to a page detailing the delivery charges. At this point, if the cost is too high, you have the option to empty your basket or find another book.
- The **Checkout** button, or similar option, opens a final page where you can complete a form with your details and then confirm the purchase.

Security

Before you have to pay for the goods, well-designed sites will open a new window that confirms the site is secure (see Figure 8.1). This means that any details provided will be encrypted – ie converted into code so that no-one else can read them – and you can feel comfortable entering your credit card details. If such a security alert is *not* provided, you may decide to stop at this point and place your order over the telephone or in writing, although these methods are not necessarily safer. Normally a symbol such as a padlock will appear at the bottom of your screen when you are viewing secure pages, and you will be told when you are about to leave the area.

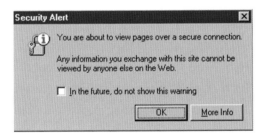

Figure 8.1

Some sites will send confirmation to you by email, but in case there is a problem, and certainly when the purchase price is very high, it is a good idea to print or save the final page and definitely make a note of any order numbers for future reference.

Before buying something more expensive than a book, or using a site without a high-street presence, it is recommended that you also check for contact addresses and telephone numbers and read the small print concerning returns or the complaints procedure.

133

Auctions

An adventurous way to go shopping is to take part in an online auction. Sellers place items in the auction, usually with a reserve price, and anyone wanting to buy can put in a bid stating the maximum they will pay. Email is used to let you know the state of play and whether someone else has placed a higher bid, or if the auction has finished and the goods are yours.

Honesty is clearly vital or no-one would ever use the auction again, and auction sites such as **www.ebay.com** have a system of feedback where buyers rate the dealings they have had with sellers.

Holidays

In the past, booking a holiday meant collecting heavy brochures from the travel agents, comparing prices, searching for suitable accommodation and then sitting in the office while they checked whether your chosen holiday was available on the dates you wanted to travel. Now you can do this and much more on the Web.

For anyone wanting a last-minute holiday, there are a number of sites aiming to provide this service, such as **www.bargainholidays.com**, **www.lastminute.com** and **www.thefirstresort.com** (see Figure 8.2). You are asked to select a destination, dates, and sometimes airport, and then you can choose from a list of holidays, booking direct or phoning the company if you prefer.

Sometimes you may want to use the Web to read brochures online – just enter the likely company URL in the Address box (eg **www.saga.co.uk**) and you will access Web pages covering all the normal holiday information as well as details of availability and booking forms.

If you don't mind which company you travel with, but want to visit a particular resort, using a search engine should provide details of possible sites. For example, keying in *Cyprus holidays* resulted in a long list of tour operators, including **www.cyprus-holidays.com** and **www.attica-holidays-cyprus.com**

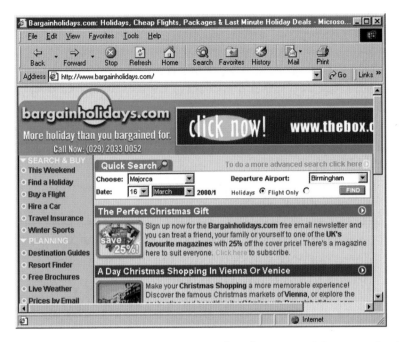

Figure 8.2 (published by permission of Online Travel Corporation)

Before choosing a holiday destination, most of us like to know what there is to see and do. Once again, search engines offer links to sites, such as **www.lonelyplanet.lycos.com** or **www.interknowledge.com**, that provide detailed information about the history, culture, country-side, and food and drink of different countries.

Other resources for the traveller include:

- weather reports (eg at **www.weather.com**)
- maps (eg at **www.cosmosnet.net**)
- travel insurance (eg from **www.insure-it.co.uk** or **www.go.com**)

Finance

A major revolution resulting from the development of the Internet has taken place within financial services. More and more banks have moved business onto the Web, and you can now buy and sell shares or invest your money in other ways over the Internet.

135

Banking

Most high street banks and building societies now have Web sites. There are also new types of bank, such as Egg or Smile, that don't have a high street presence but still operate very like conventional banks and may offer good rates of interest.

If you get in touch with your bank and it offers an online service that you would like to use, it will send you a username and password or new PIN number and you will be able to access the site and check your balance or pay bills whenever you like.

It can be a slow process, sometimes, as there is great emphasis on log-in procedures, but once you start to use the site it should be straightforward to access normal banking services.

As banks deal with money, site security is taken very seriously, but always remember that the Internet can never guarantee 100% safety for any transaction.

You may also want to make use of a new Girobank bill payment service at **www.billpayment.co.uk** if you have a debit card – you can pay your household bills online rather than going to a bank or paying by post (see Figure 8.3).

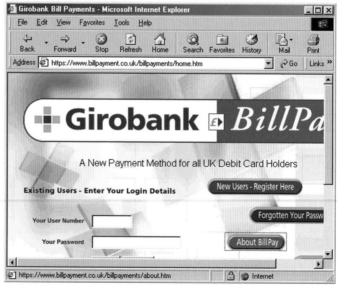

Figure 8.3 (published by permission of Alliance & Leicester)

Shares

Newcomers to the world of finance should always take professional advice before venturing into online share dealing. You can follow stories in a financial newspaper such as *The Financial Times* at **www.ft.com**, or start by visiting one of the advisory Web sites such as **www.moneyextra.com** or The Motley Fool **www.fool.co.uk** (see Figure 8.4). Both sites aim to help newcomers understand Internet finances and start share dealing.

Figure 8.4 (published by permission of The Motley Fool)

At the Motley Fool site, for example, you can read all about banking and investments, build an imaginary portfolio to practise your share dealing skills and join in discussions on a wide range of financial topics.

If you are used to dealing with stockbrokers or you manage your own portfolio of bonds and investment accounts, the great advantage of the Internet is that you can compare prices or monitor the progress of your shares instantaneously, and buying and selling is considerably quicker. As well as the sites already mentioned, others you may like to visit include **www.gomez.com** and **www.proshare.org.uk**

Learning online

There is no limit to the subjects you can learn about on the Internet. Sometimes the instructions are text-based and might be more useful in a book you could carry around with you, but many have the advantage of interactive demonstrations, attractive colour pictures and photos and links to related sources of information – and you can always print out copies if you prefer.

Short tutorials

Entering the phrase *watercolour tutorial* into the Google search engine query box, for example, yielded a list of over 200 sites. In the same way you can find sites showing you how to do anything from crocheting to speaking Spanish, practising origami, playing bridge, using a digital camera, or wiring a plug.

If you always include words such as *tutorial*, *guides*, *master class* or *tips* in the query box, you should avoid sites that are trying to sell you equipment or books on the topic of interest.

As well as using search engines, you may find a more limited, and therefore manageable, list of sites displayed if you follow up category headings on a directory site. *Don't* follow up the *Education* heading, however, as this will simply result in lists of colleges and schools. Instead, select the appropriate category (eg *Leisure and Recreation* or *Computing*) and then click sub-headings on your area of interest until you can search the list of sites for tutorials. (If you know of a specialist gateway, as explained in the last chapter, this is likely to be a particularly fruitful starting point when searching for tutorials on a specific topic.)

Some useful tutorial or educational sites that cover a wide range of subjects or offer links to specialist sources of help include:

- **www.tvchannel.co.uk/knowledge/**
- **www.thegateway.org**
- **www.about.com**
- **www.free-ed.net**

- www.thirdage.com/learning
- www.educationworld.com

Courses

Rather than a self-help tutorial, you may be interested in taking a longer course that could even lead to a diploma or other qualification. More and more educational establishments have now realised that home-based learning appeals to a wide range of adults who haven't the time, or interest, in becoming full-time students, and former correspondence courses are slowly being transferred onto the Internet.

The most well known university to develop distance learning courses is the Open University at **www.open.ac.uk** It offers a mix of computer, audio and paper delivery of courses, including one on the subject of IT that is entirely Internet-based. Continuing Education Departments at other universities such as Exeter and Oxford have also put some of their courses onto the Internet and you can now study local history, law or computing in this way.

To find out about distance learning courses, either contact the universities direct or visit their Web sites at **www.(name).ac.uk** You could also search the database of courses held by Learn Direct at **www.learndirect.org.uk** (for further details of this service see page 175).

Sharing an interest

With a computer in the home, there is no need to feel isolated. People with similar interests are waiting to 'meet' you and have a discussion or even heated debate, or they may prefer to learn from your expertise or offer you their advice and answer any specific queries.

Forums and chat rooms

On many of the sites that you visit, you will see labels in the index that refer to forums or chat rooms and you may also come across message boards. When you access a forum or message board you can read messages that have been sent in on the topic under discussion and if you follow the instructions you can add your own comments.

Chat rooms make fuller use of the Internet's interactive facilities as you can have an almost instantaneous exchange of views with people online at the same time simply by typing into the box provided. You usually have to register to enter chat rooms (although this is free and very quick) and provide an identity by which others can address you, but then taking part in the discussion will seem almost as real as speaking directly to other people in the 'room'.

Finding chat rooms is very easy as all you need do is enter your interest area + 'chat' in any search engine query box. One for older surfers can be found at **www.lifebegins.net** Age Resource, which is part of Age Concern, offers a chat site called the Baby Boomer Bistro at **www.bbb.org.uk**

Newsgroups

Newsgroups are discussion groups where members who share a common interest can exchange ideas via email. Many are perfectly legitimate and informative, but do bear in mind that some strange people use the Internet and you may not like everything you read (this applies equally to chat rooms).

When people send in their views, referred to as 'articles', these are then posted out to other members of the group and can be answered by anyone who wants to join in. The messages sent to newsgroups are stored on computers known as 'news servers' that are part of the Usenet computer network, and your ISP usually provides links to one or more. Details of how to join a newsgroup can be found in the next chapter on pages 156–157.

Keeping informed

If you don't mind reading from a computer screen rather than the printed page, you can now get your up-to-date news and comment from the Web by visiting the sites of major TV companies or UK and international newspapers and magazines (eg **www.sportinglife.com** or **www.guardian.co.uk**). In some cases the complete newspaper appears to have been published on the Web, but most organisations have created online versions that take more account of the different format.

Apart from current affairs, there is so much information on the Web that a list of interesting sites would take a book in itself. Everyone has different interests but here are a few examples to start you off. You can:

- view weather reports on sites such as **www.yahoo.com/weather**
- find maps on sites such as **www.streetmap.co.uk** or **www.ordnancesurvey.co.uk**
- look up train timetables at **www.railtrack.co.uk**
- check spellings at **www.onelook.com**
- consult the online Encyclopaedia Britannica at **www.eb.com** for information on almost anything (only trial searches are available free – for full searches you have to pay a subscription)
- find out how things work at **www.howstuffworks.com**
- discover the address or phone number of an elusive business by using the online *Yellow Pages* directory at **www.yell.com**

Printed versions of magazines are now very helpful for locating Web pages. In copies of any magazine about computers, or covering a special interest such as crafts, golf or gardening, you will see Web site addresses listed alongside articles and advertisements. It's a good idea to start noting these down for when you go online. If the Web pages appeal and you find them helpful, add them to your Favourites folders and they will remain easily accessible for future online sessions.

Playing music

Thousands of songs and music scores are now available on the Internet in a compressed format known as MP3. The MP3 versions will be very close to CD quality and you can play them directly when connected to the Internet, or you may prefer to download and store them on your computer or even buy a portable MP3 player so that you can take your music with you when you are away from home.

Most new computers should have the software on them to play MP3 files, but if you haven't got a new computer and you double-click the file and it won't play, you can find free versions of MP3 players such as *WinAmp* on the Internet that will download in a few minutes. Links to players are available on the same sites you visit to find music.

A good site to start at is **www.mp3.com** but you can use any search engine to locate music if you type in the singer or composer's name, the music title and the word *download*. Once you have located a piece of music you can often click the play button to hear it immediately. To save it to play offline, click the download button and wait for it to be transferred onto your hard disk. Single songs can take about 10 minutes, so bear in mind you will have to be patient if you want to store a complete symphony.

Games

Computer games are not all violent or child-orientated, and you can find thousands of free games to download and play or you can connect to the Internet and play online with other people.

You will already have a few games installed with Windows and these can be found by opening the Start – Programs – Accessories – Games menu. To play, open the game and, if necessary, first read the rules by clicking Help.

To add to your repertoire, connect to the Internet and search for games to download. One excellent site is **http://shareware.cnet.com** and there are clear instructions for downloading the program files onto your computer. ('Shareware' refers to programs that have been made widely available for free or at very low cost.)

If you want to play online, good sites include **www.funster.com** or **www.pogo.com**. You will need to register but then you can choose your game and play for free (see Figure 8.5).

For advice, or to contribute a game or puzzle, you can make use of any forums or enter a games chat room that may be available on the site.

Figure 8.5 (published by permission of Electronic Arts)

Sites for the Over 50s

As well as the Age Concern site (**www.ageconcern.org.uk**), there are a number of other UK sites that have been established specifically for the more mature Internet surfer. They fall into three broad categories: those published by organisations such as charities that are there to provide advice and campaign on behalf of older people; sites with the limited aim of providing hyperlinks to other sources of information; and more entertainment-based sites that offer a mix of magazine-style articles, news, chat rooms or forums, and some advertising of relevant books, equipment, holidays or financial advice, etc:

- **www.laterlife.co.uk** (magazine-style)
- **www.idf50.co.uk** (standing for *I don't feel 50* and mainly offering links)
- **www.silversurfers.net** (links to related sites)
- **www.lifes4living.co.uk** (magazine-style)
- **www.retirement-matters.co.uk** (magazine-style)

- **www.twilightyears.co.uk** (magazine-style)
- **www.helptheaged.org.uk** (charity)
- **www.lifebegins.net** (magazine and chat)
- **www.hairnet.org** (meeting place and emphasis on computer training)

Every site will offer some links to others on related topics so that a half-hour browse could result in a huge bank of resources that you can draw on whenever you need help with an issue related to being over 50.

You can find listings of other relevant sites in the Age Concern publication *How to Be a Silver Surfer* (see page 178).

Email

Email stands for electronic mail and is the method for sending messages from your computer to another linked through the Internet. As you only need to connect when you are sending or receiving messages, it can be a very cheap means of communication, with the phone call normally lasting just a few seconds.

Unlike a telephone conversation, the people you write to don't need to be anywhere near their computers when you send your message. Messages are stored on a distant computer known as the 'server', and waiting emails are delivered whenever anyone clicks their **Send and Receive** button.

This chapter explains how to use email. It looks at:

- Email addresses
- Different email systems
- Mailboxes and folders
- Writing an email
- Sending your message
- Receiving messages
- Attachments
- Address Books
- Organising your messages
- Newsgroups
- Spam

Email addresses

An email address consists of a username, the symbol @ and then the domain name of the recipient's server. For example:

john.mitchell@virgin.net or **today@bbc.co.uk**

There is no equivalent to the telephone directory and so finding someone's email address can be difficult. If you cannot contact them by other means to get their correct address, you can try using the people-finding directories built into Windows and accessed via the Start – Find – People menu, but it is very much a hit and miss option.

As with everything on the Internet, the exact address must be typed accurately. If it is not, you will soon get a message from the administrator of the service saying that the email was not delivered.

Different email systems

There are two basic systems you could use: software installed on your own computer (eg Outlook Express, Eudora or some ISP-customised systems that should all be available offline for most of the time); or a free email service offered from a Web site such as **www.hotmail.com** or **www.yahoo.com** that you have to connect to in order to use.

To use a Web-based system, you register by going to the Web site and filling in a short questionnaire to include a choice of username and password. Each time you want to read, compose, send or receive messages, you first 'log in' by entering these details.

It is clearly cheaper if you have a computer at home to use systems such as Outlook Express. You can always register with a Web-based service if you are away from home a great deal, or you don't have your own computer and need to access emails in different countries or from different places such as a computer club or Internet cafe. (Outlook Express will even allow you to set up an account that offers access to your emails from different computers, and you can find out how to do this from the Help menu).

As the different email systems work in a similar way, this book explains how to use Outlook Express, and you should then find it quite simple to use any other system provided by your ISP or Web-based service.

Mailboxes and folders

When you first open Outlook Express (see Figure 9.1), you will see a general contents page, including a Tip of the day, and you can open any of the folders in the left-hand pane to view their contents by clicking their name. At the bottom of the main page click the checkbox if you want to set the system to open your incoming mail folder – the Inbox – automatically when Outlook Express starts.

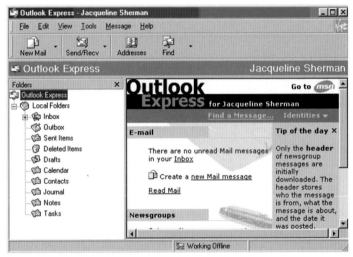

Figure 9.1

If the **Dial-up Connection** box appears, click **Work Offline** to save paying for reading and thinking time. (You will also need to close the window that appears saying checking for messages couldn't take place.)

The main folders you will open regularly are:

Inbox – all new messages arrive here and will remain until you move or delete them.

Outbox – when you send a message (or select the option to send it later), it will be stored here until you connect to the Internet.

Sent Items – this holds copies of any messages that have been sent.

Deleted Items – messages you don't want are stored here until you empty the folder.

Drafts – you can save any messages here, and then send or work on them later, if you select File – Save instead of clicking the Send button.

Writing an email

If you click the **New Mail** button (which may be labelled *Compose* or *Create* in other systems) you will open a composing window (see Figure 9.2). There are boxes in which to enter the email addresses of people receiving the original (*To:*) or copies (*Cc:*) of the message, and a *Subject:* box. Try to type a brief but clear title here that will make someone want to read your message (*Report* is far less intriguing than *Fantastic news*, for example).

Click to send straightaway
or as soon as you go online

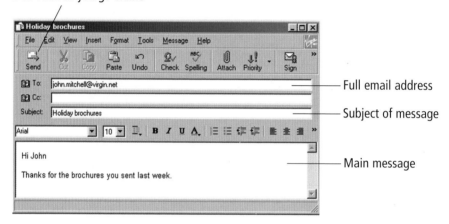

Full email address

Subject of message

Main message

Figure 9.2

You won't need to put your own email address as this is added auto-matically.

In the main window, you can type your message just as you would write a letter, although emails tend to be rather less formal and many people start with *Hi* or *Hello* rather than *Dear* …. You won't need to worry about the look of your message, as most email systems don't support ornate and complex formatting. (To send an attractively word-processed message, it is best to keep it in its original format and send it as an attachment as described on pages 151–153.)

Before you send or store your message, click the Spelling button to carry out a quick spellcheck, as the cautionary red or green wavy lines you find appearing in Word will not appear in an email message.

Sending your message

Having finished writing your message, select File – Send Later if you are creating several messages, so that they are all stored temporarily in your outgoing mailbox. Otherwise, click the Send button. If you are already connected to the Internet, the message will be sent instantly. If not, you will be reminded that you need to connect and the message will be placed, ready, in your Outbox.

When a message disappears from the Outbox and can be found in your Sent folder, you can assume that it has reached the correct server – although you won't know if or when it arrives in someone's Inbox until and unless you get a reply.

Receiving messages

One slightly annoying feature of the system is that, if you click the Send button after writing a message, you won't necessarily receive mail at the same time. To see if any messages have arrived for you since you last checked, you need to be connected to the Internet and click the Send and Receive button on the main toolbar. If there are any messages for you, you will see a number appear next to the Inbox folder showing new, unread messages, and there will be a message at the bottom of the screen saying how many messages have arrived.

Opening the Inbox (see Figure 9.3) will reveal the messages that have been sent to you. You can see details of the sender together with the subject of the message, and can scroll through the text of any selected messages in a preview pane below. Double-clicking any message will open it fully on screen in its own window.

Reply to incoming message

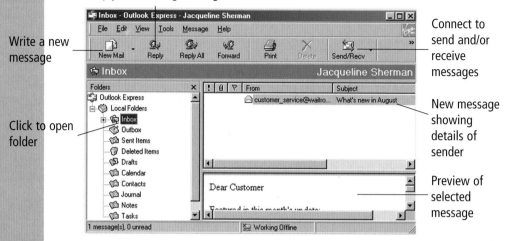

Write a new message

Click to open folder

Connect to send and/or receive messages

New message showing details of sender

Preview of selected message

Figure 9.3

Replying and forwarding

The quick way to reply to someone is to select the message and click the **Reply** button. You will then see a composing box with their name already entered in the *To:* box and the subject of their message, preceded by *Re:*, in the Subject box (see Figure 9.4).

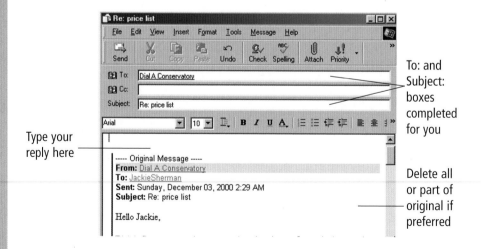

To: and Subject: boxes completed for you

Type your reply here

Delete all or part of original if preferred

Figure 9.4

You can either delete the original message (which shows in the main message window), or leave all or part of it there as a reminder. Add your comments where the cursor is flashing and then treat it just like a normal outgoing email.

The Reply All button should only be clicked if you can see from the *Cc:* box that you are on a mailing list and you want everyone else, as well as the sender of the message, to read your reply.

Forwarding a message to someone else is also easy: click the Forward button and add their address in the *To:* box and your comments on the message in the main window. You will notice that the *Subject:* box is already completed for you and this time contains the original title preceded by *Fw:*.

Attachments

As long as you create and save documents or pictures using commonly available software packages, you should be able to send them as 'attachments' to your emails and they should be easy for other people to open and view. Documents created in Word, for example, or saved in a simplified format known as Rich Text Format (.rtf) should be fine. Image files that are commonly used on computers include JPEG (.jpg), GIF (.gif) and Bitmap (.bmp).

The advantage of attaching files is that all the formatting, colours or layouts will be maintained, as the file will open up in an appropriate application when it is received. Attachments are ideal, for example, if you want to send photos of a new baby or a family wedding to relatives and friends overseas. You can do this almost as soon as the event takes place as long as you have a digital camera available.

To send your attachment, start composing your new message and then click the Attachment button (see Figure 9.5).

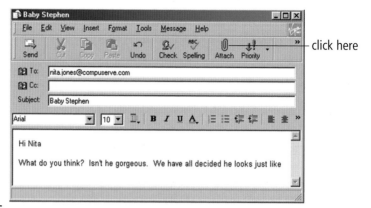

click here

Figure 9.5

You can now look through your files until you find the correct picture, select it and click *Attach* (see Figure 9.6).

Select file ——

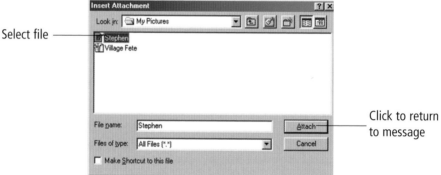

Click to return
to message

Figure 9.6

Back in your message, you will see a new box has opened displaying details of the attached file. You can attach further files in the same way before sending the message (see Figure 9.7).

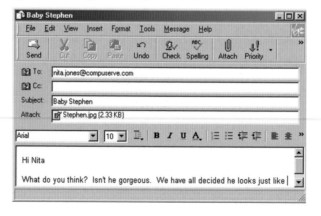

Figure 9.7

When you receive mail, you can tell that a message has an attachment as it displays a paperclip symbol 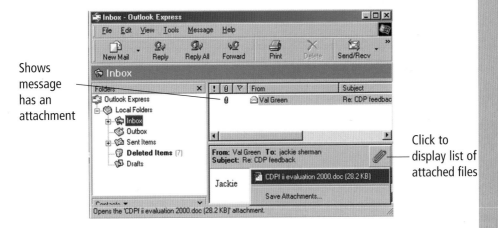. To open an attachment, you can either fully open the message and double-click the filename in the *Attach* box, or you can preview the message and click the paperclip symbol that appears in the corner. This will drop down a list of the attachments and you can select any to open (see Figure 9.8).

Shows message has an attachment

Click to display list of attached files

Figure 9.8

Address Books

Once you start using emails, you will find there are certain people you write to regularly. As with a normal address book, you can store email addresses; because they are on your computer you will also be able to insert them automatically into your messages.

When you want to add the address of someone who has written to you, find their email in the Inbox and *right*-click the name in the *From* column. Select *Add Sender to Address Book*. If you have replied to them before, your system may be set up to add addresses automatically, so that you may get a message to say this has been done. (If you want to set up your system to do this, go to **Tools – Options – Send** and click the box that says *Automatically put people I reply to in my Address Book*.)

Very often, someone new will give you their email address in person or you'll find it on a card or letter. To add their details, click the **Addresses** button 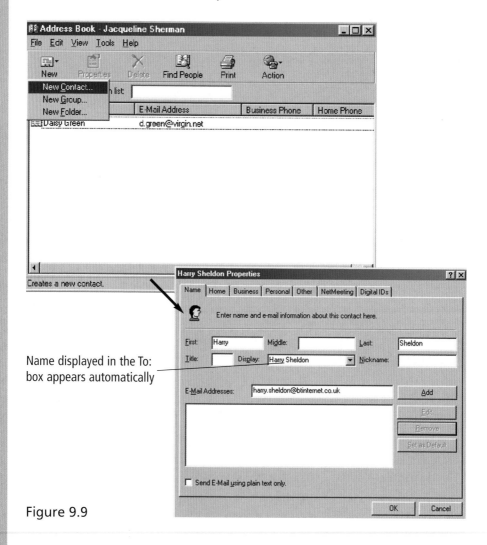, or go to **Tools – Address Book**, to open the Address Book window. Click *New – New Contact* and complete the name and email boxes (see Figure 9.9). When you click **Add** and **OK**, the new email address will be added to your Address Book list.

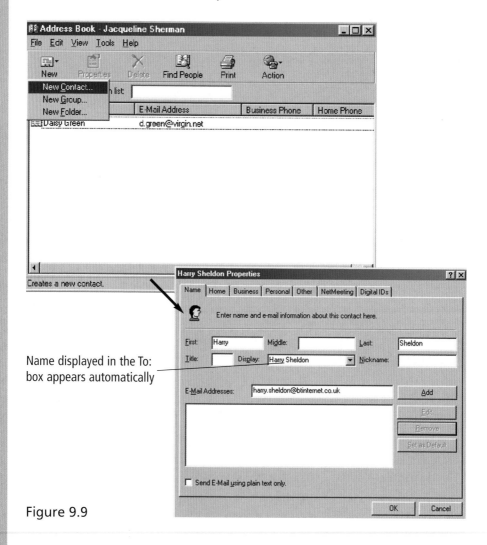

Name displayed in the To: box appears automatically

Figure 9.9

For your next message to someone in your Address Book, click the book symbol next to the *To:* box in the new message window, find their name and click the *To:* or *Cc:* button to add the address to the correct box (see Figure 9.10). Click **OK** to return to your message.

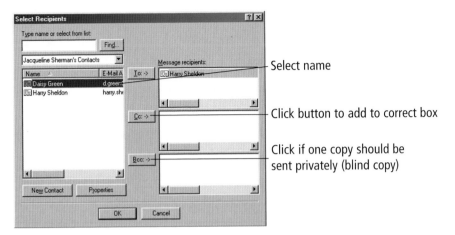

Select name

Click button to add to correct box

Click if one copy should be
sent privately (blind copy)

Figure 9.10

You can also start entering an email address in the *To:* box as this will
often bring up the details of people in your address book whose names
start with the letter(s) you type.

Organising your messages

It is not a good idea to leave all your messages in the Inbox as you will
find it hard to see which emails are new, and even harder to locate an
old message when you need to.

Just like file management in Windows Explorer, you can make folders
inside your Inbox and keep your messages organised inside them. Do
this by selecting the Inbox and going to File – New – Folder (or File –
Folder – New) and naming the folder that appears. To move messages
into your new folders, either drag them (see page 16) across the window
from right to left pane, or select each one (or a range/several individual
messages whilst holding down Shift/Ctrl) and *right*-click to obtain a
Move to Folder (or Copy to Folder) menu option. Click the correct
folder in the window that appears and click OK.

Messages can also be treated like any other files – use the File menu
options to print copies or save them in suitable folders on your hard
disk.

155

Find your messages by expanding the Inbox folders structure (see page 15), open the appropriate folder and view its contents in the right pane of the Outlook Express window.

As well as organising messages, it is vital to delete any you are sure you won't want to read again. Just select them and press the Delete key. They will actually be placed in the Deleted Items folder so that, if you make a mistake, you can open the folder and move them out again. Don't forget to use the *Edit* menu to delete the contents of this folder altogether from time to time, however.

Newsgroups

As mentioned in the last chapter, there are thousands of newsgroups devoted to different subject areas and you can take part in their discussions using your email system or through a Web-based site such as **www.deja.com/usenet**

Once you have joined your chosen newsgroup(s) you will be sent copies of recent articles when you go online, but can then disconnect to read them and respond as and when you like. You can choose to reply to just the author of the article or to everyone in the group.

Before posting your first article it's a good idea to check the advice provided on newsgroup rules (known as 'netiquette') as well as to read any articles entitled FAQs – frequently asked questions. As anyone is free to join a newsgroup, some have 'moderators' who check and filter out articles that they regard as unacceptable.

If you want to join your first newsgroup on the topic of antiques, for example, first open Outlook Express and click Set up a Newsgroups account or go to Tools – Newsgroups to link to a news server provided by your ISP and download a list of all the newsgroups held there.

Now if you enter *antiques* in the *Display newsgroups which contain …* box you should see a list of all the groups that contain this word and you can choose one or more to join (see Figure 9.11).

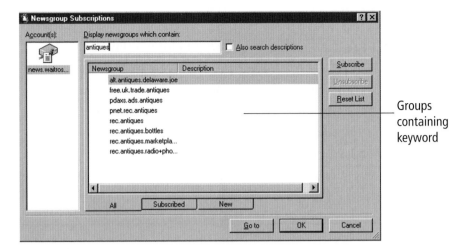

Groups
containing
keyword

Figure 9.11

To help decide which groups would suit you best, note that they usually belong to a particular category, such as:

- *rec* (recreational activity groups);
- *alt* (alternative-style groups);
- *sci* (scientific groups);
- *misc* (miscellaneous groups that don't fit into the main categories):
- *comp* (computing groups); or
- *uk* (relevant to UK-based members).

Before joining, have a look at the messages that are being posted by clicking the **Go to** button. The email news messages will appear in your Outlook Express window for previewing and reading in the same way as normal emails.

It is free to join and it doesn't involve any commitment on your part. If you are interested, click the **Subscribe** button (or double-click the newsgroup name). A new newsgroup folder will be opened automatically in Outlook Express and recent articles will be saved here whenever you connect to the news server. If you change your mind, just click the **Unsubscribe** button and the folder will be removed.

Spam

Before leaving this chapter, you may find it helpful to know how to cut down on the junk mail ('spam') that you are likely to receive, especially if you have a Web-based email address. In Outlook Express, you will find a **Block Sender** option on the **Message** menu so that selected mail in your Inbox can be added to a list of addresses whose future messages will be blocked. For other systems, see if you have a similar option, or contact the administrator for advice. In this way you should receive only messages that you will want to read.

Chapter 10

Creating your own Web site

An interesting and enjoyable activity is to design and publish your own Web site. Perhaps you would like to promote your village, or you may want to advertise handcrafted goods, or provide information about an enterprise in which you are involved. It is really very easy to do and, with most Internet service providers, free as well. This chapter explains how to go about it, describing:

- Planning your site
- Using HTML
- Creating Web pages in Frontpage Express (including saving, formatting, hyperlinks, images and different views of your page)
- Checking the site
- Publishing on the Web

Planning your site

Every page that you access on the World Wide Web was created originally as a file on someone's computer. When large numbers are grouped together and linked to one another, they form a Web site. To be visible and work via hyperlinks, each page has to be saved as an HTML (HyperText Markup Language) file, although they can be created using commonly available applications such as Word or Notepad. After creating all your Web pages, these are 'uploaded' (ie transferred to your service provider's computer to be stored). Your Web site will have a URL and can then be accessed by anyone surfing the Web.

Although you can create a Web page at any time, a serious Web site needs to be designed on paper first. This is because, rather like a family tree, the links and branches are important. For the site to be easy to navigate, you need to keep text minimal and links clear and logical.

You could practise by creating an Older Surfers Site, for example. Try to think about what pages you could include and how they would link up. In the example below (see Figure 10.1), only six pages have been defined, but your own Web site could have many more.

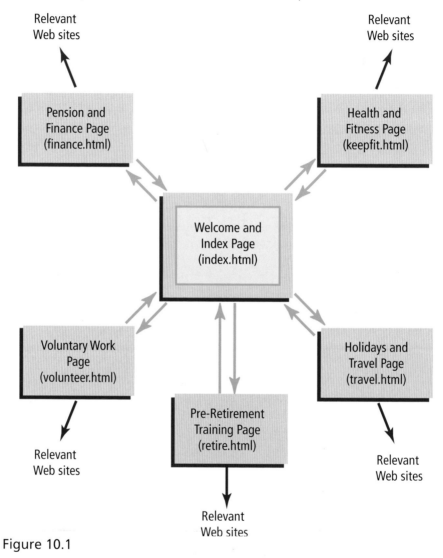

Figure 10.1

Each of the six pages needs to be designed as a separate HTML file, but saved into the same folder on your computer. Any background patterns and pictures that will be saved as separate image files should also be stored in the same folder. This will allow you to refer to them simply by their filenames and transfer them all onto the Web in one go.

The main page is created in exactly the same way as the others, but has to be saved with the filename *index.htm* (or *html*, depending on the Web authoring software). On the Web, this will then be the page opened first when anyone enters your URL in the address/location box. (Sometimes visitors will enter the exact filename of another page – for example URL/*keepfit.htm* – but this is usually as a result of discovering the page and noting its filename to pass on or return to another day.)

Using HTML

HTML files use a code that is written into each page, instructing the browser how to display the information that is contained. Although web authoring packages such as Microsoft FrontPage, Adobe PageMill and Netscape Composer allow you to create Web pages without any knowledge of the code, it is a good idea to understand at least the basic structure so that you can have more control over any changes you want to make to your pages. (There are many books available on designing Web pages so this chapter will just cover the main features.)

Some essential facts about HTML code are:

- Instructions are called *tags* and are usually in pairs, placed before (opening) and after (closing) each section of the page contents.
- Tags are often written in capitals, and are enclosed within chevrons (angled brackets) – for example <TITLE>. There should be no spaces in the tag.
- Closing tags are the same as opening tags except for / in front of the code – for example <TITLE>My Home Page</TITLE>
- Web pages have two main sections: the *head* that contains background information about the page, such as the fact that it is written in HTML and the name that will be displayed in the browser's title bar and someone's Favourites folder; and the *body* that contains everything you actually see on screen when you access a Web page.

■ Tags and their attributes (eg italic or centre alignment) are essential for all layout and formatting instructions, as the browser won't otherwise recognise such things as new paragraphs, formatted text or hyperlinks.

If, for example, your Keep Fit page included details of a local evening class you were offering, and you wanted a heading across the top, you can see quite a difference between the page in the 'raw' state, and when displayed within a browser window (see Figure 10.2).

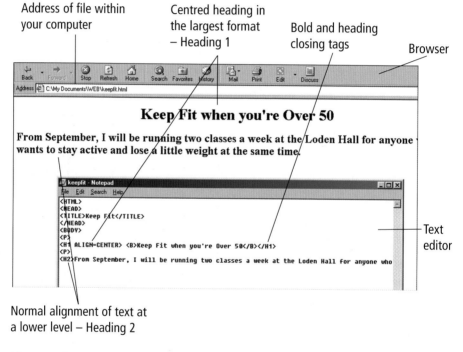

Address of file within your computer

Centred heading in the largest format – Heading 1

Bold and heading closing tags

Browser

Text editor

Normal alignment of text at a lower level – Heading 2

Figure 10.2

Whenever you access a page on the Web, you can always view (but never change) the HTML source in the browser window by selecting View – Source. It is a good idea to look at other Web sites to see how they have used HTML.

Basic HTML code

Some of the most common tags and attributes are listed below. Those marked * do not usually require a closing tag:

<HTML> Start of HTML page	<HEAD> Beginning of head section
<TITLE> Page title to display across top of browser window	<BODY> Beginning of body section
<...LINK="colour"> Within <BODY>, this sets the colour for hyperlink text	* Start on a new line
*<P> Start a new paragraph	*<HR> Horizontal line across the page
<H1> The top level of heading	<H6> The lowest level of heading
<B> Format text to bold	*<...ALIGN=CENTER> Within another tag, centres the text
<A> A hyperlink	<A HREF="filename"> The page opened when the hyperlink is clicked
*<IMG SRC="filename"> Inserts an image file	<A MAILTO="email address"> Opens a new message box addressed to the named person
"#FFFFFF" code for white – most colours are entered as codes	"Black" One of 16 colours where the name is accepted

Creating Web pages in FrontPage Express

You can buy full versions of Web authoring software, but there are free cut-down versions available that are perfectly adequate for beginners. One such package is Microsoft FrontPage Express. It may already be installed on your computer; if not, it can be downloaded from the Microsoft Web site (**www.microsoft.com**). The toolbars and menus will look quite familiar, although there are several special features you can use.

To produce a welcome page using FrontPage Express, you should open the application and, on a new blank page, type in the following (or your own choice of text):

Older Surfers' Site

Welcome to this new Web site. I hope you will find it fun and informative. Follow the links to discover what we can offer, and what else is available on the Web.

Saving

Click the **Save** button and, in the box that appears, enter your own choice of Page Title to display in the browser title bar. Then click the **As File** button and save it as *index*. To keep your files together, you could first create a new folder to save it into (eg *Older surfers*).

Now type the following list and add bullets by selecting the text and clicking the **Bullets** toolbar button ▤ :

■ *Go to Finance to find out how to look after your money.*
■ *Keep fit and active with advice on our Health page.*
■ *Discover the joys of travel by booking one of the specialist holidays listed on our Travel page.*
■ *Book yourself a pre-retirement training course if you need to find out how to make the best of your spare time by turning to our Pre-Retirement page.*
■ *Help the community by becoming a volunteer – full details on the Volunteer page.*

Formatting

To make the heading stand out, select the text and choose a high level heading, such as *Heading1* from the **Style** box list (see Figure 10.3). Then centre it and change the font type or select a colour from the *Text Color* palette.

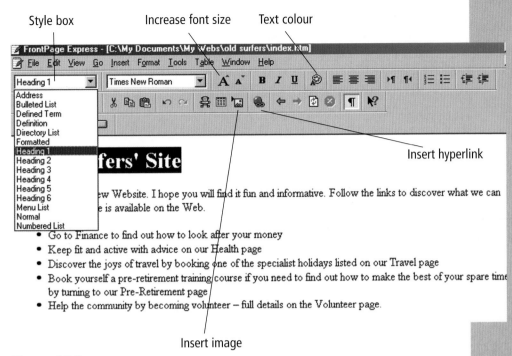

Style box   Increase font size   Text colour

Insert hyperlink

Insert image

Figure 10.3

Overall background colour is easy to add – select this from the **Format** – **Background** dialog box and choose a named colour or click **Custom** and mix your own.

You will see that the colours of hyperlinks in your page are pre-set but can be altered, and you could add a picture or pattern as your background if you enter the image filename in the box provided.

You can now incorporate other features. For example, you can add a horizontal line from the **Insert** menu and change its attributes by *right-clicking* and choosing different widths and heights.

Hyperlinks

To link your index to further pages on your site, or other locations on the Web, you need to add hyperlinks.

Select the text that will be clicked (eg *Finance* in the first list item), and then open the *Create Hyperlink* box via the **Insert** – **Hyperlink** menu or by clicking the toolbar button 🍋. This is where you can link several pages that are open at the same time; create a new page straightaway; or insert a range of different links by clicking the World Wide Web tab. You can select:

- *http:* for a link to a Web page;
- *mailto:* to add an email link; or
- *file:* to link to other files on your computer.

Although not yet created, select *file:* and enter *finance.htm* in the URL box as you will eventually be creating and saving this file into your Web folder (see Figure 10.4).

Link to an
open page:

Click on file: as
the type of link

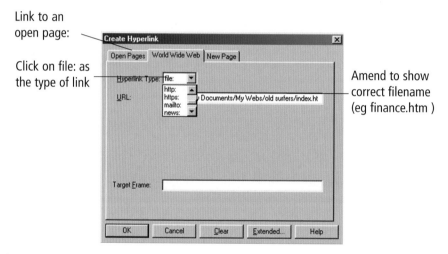

Amend to show
correct filename
(eg finance.htm)

Figure 10.4

Back in your document, Finance is now blue and underlined, and you can repeat the process with all text entries that link to other pages on your site.

For links to other sites, select relevant clickable text and create a link by selecting *http:* as the type of hyperlink. For example, on your Volunteer page, you could provide information about voluntary work overseas – enter and select the word VSO and insert a link by typing **http://www.vso.org.uk** in the URL box.

Images

You may also want to add a picture to your page. To display on the Web, images should be either a .jpeg or .gif file; perhaps one you have saved from the Web or scanned in.

Move or copy any images that you want to use into the folder containing your Web pages so that the file pathway is the same. Then simply click the Insert Image button ☒ or go to Insert – Image – From File and browse through your picture files to find one that is suitable.

You can now edit the picture on the page. For example, to add a border, *right*-click and select *Image Properties*.

Your page may now look something like Figure 10.5.

Older Surfers' Site

- Go to Finance to find out how to look after your money.

- Keep fit and active with advice on our Health page.

- Discover the joys of travel by booking one of the specialist holidays listed on our Travel page.

- Book yourself a pre-retirement training course if you need to find out how to make the best of your spare time by turning to our Pre-Retirement page.

- Help the community by becoming a volunteer - full details on the Volunteer page.

Figure 10.5

To build your site, create the other five pages and make sure that you save them into the same folder each time.

Different views of your page

Source code

In FrontPage Express, the HTML code is written as you format your page. To see the code, in case you want to make changes directly to it, you need to go to View – HTML. (Return to the Web layout page by clicking OK, but don't forget to save any changes you make.)

The index page would now look like Figure 10.6.

Font colour shown as code

```
<h1 align="center"><font color="#FF0000">Old Surfers' Site</font></h1>
<blockquote>
    <h3>Welcome to this new Website. I hope you will find it fun
    and informative. Follow the links to discover what we can
    offer, and what else is available on the Web.</h3>
</blockquote>
```

Horizontal line with attributes

```
<hr size="4" noshade width="78%">

<ul type="disc">
    <li class="MsoNormal"
    style="mso-list:l1 level1 lfo2;tab-stops:list 36.0pt left 361.5pt"><font
        size="4">Go to </font><a href="finance.html"><font
        size="4">Finance</font></a><font size="4"> to find out
        how to look after your money</font></li>
    <li class="MsoNormal"
    style="mso-list:l1 level1 lfo2;tab-stops:list 36.0pt left 361.5pt"><font
        size="4">Keep fit and active with advice on our </font><a
        href="keepfit.html"><font size="4">Health </font></a><font
        size="4">page</font></li>
    <li class="MsoNormal"
    style="mso-list:l1 level1 lfo2;tab-stops:list 36.0pt left 361.5pt"><font
        size="4">Discover the joys of travel by booking one of
        the specialist holidays listed on our </font><a
        href="travel.html"><font size="4">Travel </font></a><font
        size="4">page</font></li>
    <li class="MsoNormal"
    style="mso-list:l1 level1 lfo2;tab-stops:list 36.0pt left 361.5pt"><font
        size="4">Book yourself a pre-retirement training course
        if you need to find out how to make the best of your
        spare time by turning to our </font><a href="retire.html"><font
        size="4">Pre-Retirement</font></a><font size="4"> page</font></li>
    <li class="MsoNormal"
    style="mso-list:l1 level1 lfo2;tab-stops:list 36.0pt left 361.5pt"><font
        size="4">Help the community by becoming a volunteer
        &#150; full details on the </font><a
        href="volunteer.html"><font size="4">Volunteer</font></a><font
        size="4"> page.</font></li>
    <li class="MsoNormal"
    style="mso-list:l1 level1 lfo2;tab-stops:list 36.0pt left 361.5pt"><font
        size="4"></font> </li>
</ul>

<p align="center"><img src="J0101864.gif" border="3" width="248"
height="164"></p>
```

Hyperlink

Clickable text on page

New paragraph (HTML code shows as coloured rather than in capitals)

Picture file

Figure 10.6

Browser window view

Another view is available in your browser window. To see how the page looks on the Web, minimise the FrontPage Express window (see page 11) and open your browser as normal. Make sure you stay working offline, and then open the page by going to File – Open and using the Browse button to locate the file. Different browsers interpret instructions differently, and so you may notice some changes. One difference is that the hyperlink hand symbol will appear as you move the mouse over the links you have inserted, and as you design and save other pages for your site you will be able to move between them as you do on the Web.

To make changes, click the minimised **FrontPage Express file** button on the taskbar. When you return to view the page again in the browser window, make sure that you have taken into account the latest changes by saving them in FrontPage Express and clicking the **Refresh** button in the browser window.

Using other applications

If you prefer to use your word processing application to create the same pages, you can do so with very little need to write HTML, as there is a Web layout view to work in. To help you with the overall design of the site, including setting up frames that divide the pages into separate sections, you can explore the Web Wizard available via the **File – New – Web Pages** menu.

Checking the site

Once you have produced all your pages, there are some general questions you should ask yourself:

- **Do the pages take too long to download?** You may need to split up large pages, or replace large or complex images with simpler, smaller ones.
- **Can you move smoothly through the site?** You may need navigation aids on more pages, such as *Home* text or images that, when clicked, take you back to your index page, or to other pages it now seems logical to visit at this point.
- **Is there a consistent look and feel to your site?** If you chose different fonts, background colours or layouts for every page it may be a good idea to amend some of the more extreme examples or add a similar logo to each page.

Bookmarks

If you must have large pages that extend below the screen, it can be helpful to readers to add a 'bookmark' so that, at the end of the text there is a
link to click that will take them back to the top of the page. (Please note
that this is not the same as bookmarking a favourite Web page.)

Inserting a bookmark involves two separate steps:

1 In the place you want the reader to jump *to*, click in a space, or select
   some text to anchor it to, and then go to Insert – Bookmark. A box
   appears in which you now enter the name for your bookmark (eg
   top).
2 In the position where you want the clickable text that readers move
   from, type the text and then select it and insert a hyperlink as normal.
   However, instead of entering a filename or URL, you would click
   Bookmark and select from any bookmark names you had created.

The page and HTML code would now look like this:

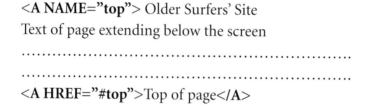

<A NAME="top"> Older Surfers' Site
Text of page extending below the screen

....

....

<A HREF="#top">Top of page</A>

Publishing on the Web

If you want to make your Web site available, you will have to publish it.
Unless you are thinking of creating a business empire, your Internet
Service Provider (ISP) is likely to be able to provide quite enough free
Web space for a small Web site. However, before you take the step of
publishing the pages, you should check that the site works properly.

Testing the links

Connect to the Internet in the normal way and then open your Web
pages via the File – Open menu. If you now click any links you have
inserted to established Web sites, you should find that they open on
screen in just the same way as when you normally browse the Web.

Make sure that there is relevant information on each site – some URLs may have come via books, magazines or word-of-mouth and sites may no longer exist – and that the Back and Forward buttons work normally. If you have two different browsers installed on your computer, check in both of these in case some images or colours look wrong.

Uploading

To place your Web pages on a host computer – the server – you will need to transfer your files. This usually involves using File Transfer Protocol (FTP). Well-known FTP programs include *CuteFTP* and WS_FTP and one of these may be provided free by your ISP if you are using their free Web space for your Web site.

You will need to open the FTP program, connect to the Internet and, initially, enter details of the username and password you used to register with your ISP.

Their site should provide full details of how to transfer your files, but most FTP programs work in a similar way. You will see two panes displayed on screen – your computer files will show in the left pane and an empty space for your Web pages will show in the right. Uploading simply involves dragging your Web pages and associated image files across from the left to the right pane. Once all files have been transferred, you should amend and replace them regularly to keep your Web site up-to-date.

Domain names

On publishing your pages, you will be told the URL of your site, and it is likely to be a rather long and awkward name.

If you think that your Web site will grow and receive hundreds of visitors, there may come a time when you want to pay for your own Web space and need a URL that is easy to remember (eg **www.oldersurfers.org.uk** or **www.oldersurfers.com**). In this case, you may have to pay to register your personal domain name, so that it will appear in search engine lists and people surfing the Web will be more

171

likely to find you. Many companies now offer this service on the Internet and will tell you if the name you have in mind is still available or is already taken.

Advertising

There are various ways to make sure that people find your Web site:

- Include the URL in any emails, letters or publicity material you send out.
- At the top of the pages, include 'meta' tags that contain keywords to help search engines pick up your pages.
- Add your URL to search engine sites – there is usually an Add URL button to click at the bottom of the page.
- Set up reciprocal mention of URLs with other sites on a similar theme, and send details to organisations or societies that might mention it in their literature.
- Send details of your Web site to newsgroups with similar interests.
- You can pay to advertise in magazines, newspapers or on other Web sites.

Chapter 11

Developing your skills

Having reached this chapter by working through some of this book, or the whole of it, you should be feeling quite confident about using your computer. If you are now also asking yourself what the next step might be, this chapter offers some suggestions, including:

- Learning through experience
- Buying books
- IT training
- CD-ROMS

Learning through experience

It is only by practising, and learning from your mistakes, that you will make real progress with the computer. Now that you have mastered the basics, you will probably want to find reasons for using your computer so that you can build up your confidence even more and, at the same time, learn new things.

The best way is by slowly moving tasks to the computer that were previously pen and paper activities – for example, you could create a Christmas presents database in Excel or party invitations in Word, help trace a family tree, or learn how to play bridge from an Internet site. You will soon find that the computer becomes the obvious place to start any such activity and that it has become indispensable.

Whatever you choose, you will find at some stage that you want to do something that isn't in this book and isn't explained by the Help menus. This is where the next option comes in.

Buying books

Most IT publications concentrate on a single package or activity, such as PowerPoint or Web page authoring. Although you could buy a book for every eventuality, realistically it is best to spend your money on a book that covers the application you are likely to use most often, or a new one that you really want to learn.

When buying computing books, it can be very hard to know which is the best one for you, especially as there are so many being produced all the time, all catering for different tastes. We all learn in different ways and some people learn best from seeing things visually, so that they may prefer a book with lots of pictures, whereas others want fuller explanations.

It is a good idea to go to the bookshop with one or two questions in mind that have either not been answered fully enough for you in this introductory book, or which are new queries – for example, how do you create your own styles in Word, or what exactly *is* desktop publishing? After looking for the answer in four or five books within your price range – and discarding any that you don't find attractive or easy to use – you will find one that seems to explain things in the clearest way. If it also covers enough new ground for you to feel that it has a reasonable shelf life, then that's the book to buy.

IT training

No book can answer all your questions fully enough or in the right amount of detail, and there really is no substitute for a personal tutor who can demonstrate how to do something or interpret the written instructions.

You should be able to find an IT course that is being offered locally at a convenient college or community hall. Some classes are now aimed at particular groups, including the over 50s, but most adult education classes cater for a wide range of ages, and tutors are very sympathetic to new computer users. Now that you have mastered some of the basics, you may have gained enough confidence to join a class or you may have decided that you can't get any further without one, and you can either study for a qualification or simply enjoy learning more whilst consolidating your skills.

Courses can be of any length – some will last a few weeks whereas others will take a year – but most of the individual sessions will last 1–2 hours at a time as concentration and stamina fall markedly if you study longer.

When choosing a course, it is very important to talk to the tutor about what you have mastered so far, so that you can pick one at an appropriate level. Some of the basic qualifications that relate to the contents of this book include CLAIT (Computer Literacy and Information Technology Stage 1), City & Guilds Level 1 or the ECDL (European Computer Driving Licence). If you already had previous computing experience, you will want to find a more advanced course that takes you further with one or more of the packages or covers completely new ground, such as programming or relational databases.

Finding a course shouldn't be too difficult. One place to start is with Learn Direct – the governmental information service that can tell you about any local courses – at **www.learndirect.co.uk** or on Freephone number 0800 100 900. You can also look at prospectuses online if you go to **www.(*name of college*). ac.uk**, or find details of adult education classes in your local library.

There are also less formal computer clubs and taster courses being run for and by older people and you may find the social atmosphere more attractive than a college. As these groups are not aiming for qualifications or offering an examination-orientated syllabus, you can learn in a more relaxed way and will have more say about what you want to study. The University of the Third Age (U3A), for example, is an organisation made up of people interested in lifelong learning who are no longer in full-time employment and who organise talks, visits and special interest groups in most areas of the UK. They may run a computer club near you and you can find out more from their Web site **www.u3a.org.uk** or by phoning 020 7837 8838. Many local Age Concerns also offer free IT taster courses, so contact them to find out more.

Private training

The convenience of having an expert coming to your home when it suits you, to show you how to use your own computer, can sometimes outweigh the extra cost and may even be cheaper than a course if they only come round once or twice. Costs will vary, but an hour's tuition fee is normally around £20.

There are tutorial services advertising in local newspapers which will check references for their home tutors, and you can always arrange for someone else to be in the house if you aren't sure you feel comfortable with strangers. One organisation – Hairnet – has developed a national network of trainers who are particularly experienced with older learners and who must be over 50 themselves. Hairnet can be located at **www.hairnet.org** or by telephone on 020 7490 2943.

CD-ROMs

A wide range of CD-ROMs is now available, usually costing between £10 and £40. A browse of the shelves should unearth CDs which show you how to type faster, learn a language, plan your garden, trace your family tree, introduce Feng Shui, draw cartoons or do many, many other things to suit all tastes and interests. Check that your computer has the appropriate memory or operating system and installation should then be a straightforward matter of inserting the CD-ROM and following the leaflet or online instructions.

Now you can see the potential of IT, it is hoped that you will continue to have fun using your machine and will derive great satisfaction from developing your computing skills.

Age Concern Information Line/Factsheets subscription
Age Concern produces 44 comprehensive factsheets. For details, telephone: 0800 00 99 66 (7am–7pm, seven days a week, every day of the year). Alternatively you may prefer to write to Age Concern, FREEPOST (SWB 30375), ASHBURTON, Devon TQ13 7ZZ.

About Age Concern

This book is one of a wide range of publications produced by Age Concern England, the National Council on Ageing. Age Concern works on behalf of all older people and believes later life should be fulfilling and enjoyable. For too many this is impossible. As the leading charitable movement in the UK concerned with ageing and older people, Age Concern finds effective ways to change that situation.

Where possible, we enable older people to solve problems themselves, providing as much or as little support as they need. A network of local Age Concerns, supported by 250,000 volunteers, provides community-based services such as lunch clubs, day centres and home visiting.

Nationally, we take a lead role in campaigning, parliamentary work, policy analysis, research, specialist information and advice provision, and publishing. Innovative programmes promote healthier lifestyles and provide older people with opportunities to give the experience of a lifetime back to their communities.

Age Concern is dependent on donations, covenants and legacies.

Age Concern England
1268 London Road
London SW16 4ER
Tel: 020 8765 7200
Fax: 020 8765 7211

Age Concern Cymru
4th Floor
1 Cathedral Road
Cardiff CF11 9SD
Tel: 029 2037 1566
Fax: 029 2039 9562

Age Concern Scotland
113 Rose Street
Edinburgh EH2 3DT
Tel: 0131 220 3345
Fax: 0131 220 2779

Age Concern Northern Ireland
3 Lower Crescent
Belfast BT7 1NR
Tel: 028 9024 5729
Fax: 028 9023 5497

How to be a Silver Surfer
A beginner's guide to the internet for the over 50s

How to be a Silver Surfer is a companion guide for people who are new to the Internet and a little apprehensive about what to do. Using simple step-by-step explanations, it helps readers through the most important tasks when first using the Internet. Topics include searching the Web, sending an email and saving a favourite Web page for future reference.

Aimed at the over 50s, the emphasis is on using the Internet as a tool to enrich existing interests, such as travel, fishing and gardening, and as a recreational activity in itself, including researching family trees, emailing family and friends, and chat sites.

This book is written in a very informal, friendly, non-technical style. Full colour illustrations and screen shots with supportive text are used extensively.

£4.99 0-86242-336-8

If you would like to order any Age Concern titles, please write to the address below, enclosing a cheque or money order for the appropriate amount (plus £1.95 p&p) made payable to Age Concern England. Credit card orders may be made on 0870 44 22 044 (for individuals/members of the public); 0870 44 22 120 (AC federation, other organisations and institutions). Fax: 01626 323318.

Age Concern Books
PO Box 232
Newton Abbot
Devon TQ12 4XQ

Glossary

Accessing Finding and opening a Web page.

Active cell The cell showing a black border, in which any data will appear when you type text or numbers. You **activate** a new cell by clicking in it with the mouse or moving there by pressing the Tab, Enter or arrow keys.

Active window When more than one window is open at the same time, this is the only window with a blue title bar in which you are able to work.

Application The named software that is dedicated to a related group of tasks, such as word processing or drawing (eg *Word* or *Publisher*).

Bitmap file A graphics (picture) file created when using an application such as *Microsoft Paint* and made up of a collection of coloured dots known as pixels.

Bookmarking Storing a favourite Web page address so that it can be opened again easily.

Browsing (see Surfing)

Browser The application that allows you to view Web pages on the World Wide Web.

CD-ROMs Shiny round disks placed on the slide-out tray in your computer that contain applications, such as encyclopaedias, games, drawing packages or music.

Cells Squares in tables or spreadsheets where you enter your data.

Central Processing Unit (CPU) The heart of your computer that controls its main functions.

Chat rooms A special kind of Web site where you can communicate in writing with other people online at the same time.

Clicking Pressing a button on your mouse to instruct the computer to carry out a particular task.

Clipboard An area of the computer memory where you temporarily store text or images before moving or copying them to another document.

Cursor A flashing black bar that marks the text insertion point.

Database Information about people or things stored in a systematic way that can be sorted or searched.

Default Settings for your work or the equipment you are using that can be accepted or changed manually.

Desktop The opening screen you see when you turn on your computer. Its name derives from the various little pictures you see that represent items in an office, such as a wastepaper basket (the Recycle Bin) or the computer itself (My Computer).

Dialog box Small windows (opened via a menu) that offer you various choices to click or type in.

Digital camera Equipment that creates digital pictures that can be viewed and stored on the computer.

Domain name Parts of a Web address that display an organisation's registered name, location and type of business.

Double-clicking Clicking the left mouse button twice very fast. It is used as a quick method to open programs or files and can be replaced by selecting the item with one click of the left mouse button and then pressing the Enter key on the keyboard.

Downloading Transferring files from the Internet onto your own computer.

Email Electronic messages sent via the Internet.

Fieldname The heading or category under which information in a database is stored.

File Piece of work – text or images – created and saved onto a computer.

File type/extension Parts of a file name showing in which application it has been produced or what type of file it is.

Floppy disk 3½" squares of plastic on which files can be stored. They can be carried around so that files can be reopened on different machines.

Folder Labelled space where you can store related programs and files.

Font Type of character used when typing text.

Formula Instructions to the computer to carry out a calculation.

FTP (File Transfer Protocol) Standard used for transferring files between computers.

Function Instructions recognised by a spreadsheet application to perform specific calculations.

Gateway Web site that can be searched for links to other sites on a single theme (eg education, health, etc).

Greyscale View of a picture that shows shades of grey instead of colours.

Hard disk Main area within the computer on which programs and files are stored.

Hardware Parts of the computer you can see and touch.

Help Demonstrations, explanations and other assistance available when working on your computer.

HTML (HyperText Mark-up Language) The code used to create Web pages.

Hyperlink Text or pictures that are embedded in Web pages and can be clicked to open related pages.

Icons Small pictures representing programs or shortcuts to common tasks.

Internet Computers around the world that are linked and can share information.

ISP (Internet Service Provider) The organisation that supplies software and facilities to allow you to link to the Internet and send emails.

IT (Information Technology) The technical term for using technology to communicate and handle information.

Jpeg file A type of graphics file that is recognised by a browser so that pictures (often photographs) can be displayed on the Web. The other common Web graphics file format is a **gif file**.

Justify Text is spread across the page to 'neaten' its appearance on the right-hand margin.

Keywords Any important words or phrases typed into a query/search box that form the basis of a search for relevant records or Web sites.

Legend Another name for the key to a chart or graph.

Log in Entering your personal name and password to access secure areas on a computer.

Mail merge Drawing information from a database so that the same document can be sent to a wide range of people and appear as if it has been addressed personally to them.

Meta tag HTML code within a Web page that includes identifying words or phrases that may help it get noticed by surfers and listed by search engines.

Modem The hardware required to allow digital computer information to travel down standard telephone lines.

Mouse Hardware that allows you to move a pointer on screen and click a button to instruct the computer to carry out a particular task.

MP3 Compressed music files.

Newsgroups Groups of people with a common interest who communicate via email.

Operating system Software controlling the general operation of the computer.

Orientation The setting you select that determines how a page is printed – either upright (**Portrait**), or turned sideways (**Landscape**) so that the longer sides are top and bottom.

Package (see Application)

PC (Personal computer) The type of computer that sits on your desk at home or work and contains most of the programs and files you use.

Placeholder An area already in place on a slide where you can insert different objects, such as charts or pictures.

Programs Ordered sets of instructions that the computer carries out.

RAM (Random Access Memory) The memory your computer uses to open and run the different applications.

Relational database An application that allows you to search for related data across a number of tables of information.

Scanner Equipment used to transfer text or images from paper onto computer.

Search engine A Web site that holds a vast database of Web pages that you search using keywords.

Server A remote computer in a networked system that houses the network operating system software along with any software applications and data files that need to be shared.

Shareware Programs or files on the World Wide Web that are either free or very cheap to use.

Shortcut A way of carrying out common tasks without needing to go through the menu options. Common shortcuts are available within each application by clicking toolbar buttons at the top of the screen.

Software The instructions, in the form of programs, that the computer needs to be able to work effectively.

Spam Unsolicited emails – similar to 'junk mail'.

Spreadsheet Text labels and numerical data created using a program that can perform calculations.

Surfing (or browsing) Describes the activity of searching the Internet for information.

Tag The general name for code words used when creating HTML files.

Taskbar The grey bar along the bottom of the screen that is always available and which houses the **Start** button, some general information such as the time and date, any minimised files and shortcuts to some of your applications or controls.

Template A file that is used to create a variety of different files based on its contents and style but that is left unaltered.

Toolbar Rows of buttons that act as shortcuts to the more common activities carried out when using your computer. Each toolbar contains a set of buttons related to a particular group of tasks, such as Drawing or Tables.

URL (Uniform Resource Locator) The address of any Web page.

Username Your identifying name for logging in, or as part of your email address.

Virus Rogue programs that damage your files and are 'caught' from infected floppy disks or via the Internet.

Web page Documents containing text, pictures, sounds, moving images etc, written in HTML, that are stored on computers around the world and can be viewed when you connect to the Internet.

Web site A collection of linked Web pages found at the same address and created by a single organisation.

Wizards Guides found in various Microsoft applications that can help you produce files or objects step-by-step.

Workbook The name given to files created in Excel. Each workbook contains a number of sheets that are saved with the file.

World Wide Web (known as **the Web** or **WWW**) All the multimedia Web pages displayed in a browser window when you connect to the Internet.

Index